THE MULES OF MONTE CASSINO

by

Jim DeFilippi

A Brown Fedora Book

Jim DeFilippi

To those who lost their lives or innocence in southern Italy during the winter of 1943-1944

And to "Rivera," Richard Conte's machine-gunning wise guy, in the best of the World War II movies, *A Walk in the Sun*.

The Mules of Monte Cassino

Hut!...
1. Italy from the South—The Battle, the Book, the Boys
2. St. Benedict's Life and the History of his Monastery
3. Jerry Builds a Meat Grinder
4. Texas Gunslingers at the Red River
5. "We're all of us mules."
6. The General Known as Petoola
7. Destruction of a Monastery
8. The Art Lovers Caravan

...Two!...

9. After the Demolition
10. Destruction of a Town
11. *Gli Sfortunati*

...Three!...

12. The Fighting Turns Feral
13. Hard Pretzels at the Alamo

...Four!...

14. A Victory Sweet, Hollow, and Slightly Drunk

...Parade...Rest!...

15. Johnny Comes Limping Home (Petoola Gets a Ride)

...At Ease...

Epilogue: Mack and Scooter Jaw on War

Bennies

> —by an anonymous G.I.

I'm blood soaked and tired,
My stomach's on fire,
Homesick, hung-over,
Lonesome, raked over,
Discharge disapproved,
And my pee's turning blue.

I've searched every sangar for a used cigarette,
My one good eye feels like a train wreck,
Can't find the pin to my last grenade,
Been deemed second choice for any First Aid.

No women, no mail,
No wine and no ale,
Lost my socks and a couple of toes,
Half of me's burning, the other half's froze.

The Krauts and the brass won't let me surrender,
Got a telephone bill with a Dear John letter,
Chewed out by a Master, chewed out by a Tech,
Doc says my nerves are a nervous wreck.

THE MULES OF MONTE CASSINO

I'm shell-shocked, sleepy, my will's be busted,
My bayonet's gone and my rifle's rusted,
My insides are twisted and all screwed up,
The mess tent is serving rancid food up.

Been wounded and neglected,
Insulted and rejected,
Best buddy's lost,
Got a maggot boss,
Sentry duty tonight,
Bomb squad tomorrow night,
Digging trenches all week,
My tent's full of leaks.

Got a touch of the dys and a touch of the clap,
I need a bath, I need a nap,
They got a mule-skinner job for me,
I was AWOL for a week or two or three,
Frostbite's grabbing more fingers and toes,
Shells from above, plate mines from below.

I shot off my foot just to get off the line.
But the medic said, "No, the other one still works fine,"
Can't leave this place till Jerry's been evicted,
Been drinking penicillin and becoming addicted.

Jim DeFilippi

My stitches came loose and need to be mended,
The whole Fifth Army just got extended,
Mess kit's frozen, I'm not getting short,
An Article 15 says I'm due in court.

My G.I. insurance cancelled due to health reasons,
My line number's cancelled due to charges of treason,
Can't find my helmet, my belt or my gun,
The latrine's off limits, I got the G.I. Runs…

And some son-of-a-bitch…
Some lifer son-of-a-bitch…
…just asked me to re-enlist.

"Hut!..."

Chapter One:
Italy from the South; The Battle, the Book, the Boys

"The conflict of the Present and the Past,
The ideal and the actual in our life,
As on a field of battle held me fast,
Where this world and the next world were at strife."

-from "Monte Cassino" by Henry Wadsworth Longfellow 1875

***

This is a story of sacrifice, slaughter, and stupidity.
Let's get started. Personally, I have never trusted anyone above the rank of E-5, so…

***

Mack: First off, this—you can't invade Italy from the south. Cannot be done.
Scooter: Once maybe, Belasarius. One time in history only.
Mack: Bell serious? Who?

Scooter: Belasarius. A few years before we got over there—536 A.D.

Mack: Yeah, that was a bit earlier on, and he was dealing, I believe, with Visigoths and Vandals, defenders who shit in their helmets, worshipped toads and ate grubs—this guy was chasing Ostrogoths out the back door—not German paratroopers who were dug in with steel plates and just waiting there for us, slick-metal proud and immovable…

Scooter: Nazis who had stubbornness inbred from centuries of paranoia.

Mack: Backed by some pom-pom waving madman/cheerleader with an Oliver Hardy mustache chanting, "Hold that line! Hold that line!"

Scooter: And, if you have a name like Belasarius I suppose you can get away with stuff like that.

***

Another military genius, Napoleon, who had been around the block a couple times militarily, pointed out, "How do you get your foot into a boot? From the top, right?" But from the south, from the heel on up? No. Better you should ride a herd of elephants over the Alps.

Generalissimo, the next time you get it into that power-puff, publicity-clogged head of yours that you want to invade *Italia* from Sicily on up, here's what you do instead. You grab hold of your federal-budget-bloated credit card (What do you got left on it? Ten billion? Twenty? A hundred billion? As many billion as you want, no limit?) and you take that plastic to the local elephant rental headquarters (Rent-a-Pachyderm?), you get yourself a herd of five-ton beauties for a month or two (One-Way Rental, to be dropped off in Salerno, weekend rates), you hold tight onto the reins, you point those big gray trunks toward *Napoli*, and you dig your spurs into two sides of elephant hide. *Giddy-yap.* That would be easier than invading Italy from the south.

***

Scooter: But old Churchy, '43, he managed to convince his Allied buddies otherwise, didn't he? Eh?
Mack: That he did. That he did.

***

My name is Henry Grif. I am an opinionated, sometimes misinformed, too often *uber*-intense military veteran who for over twenty years has been a self-employed tour guide for the battle sites of the American Civil War and the European Theater of World War II. My forehead-to-forehead lectures—sometimes seething, often, I admit, a bit incomprehensible—place the Wilderness and Monte Cassino at the nadir of American military waste and stupidity.

This is my take on the Battle of Monte Cassino, the most brutal and least known land battle of World War II.

***

Sacrifice. Slaughter. Stupidity.

The Battle for Monte Cassino, southern Italy, 1943-1944, was the most gruesome, dick-wilting, pointless, devastating battle of America's Twentieth Century, maybe in all of America's history, and that—considering the competition—is going some. The entire shit-bucket has been referred to as "five months of insanity," and if that opinion is wrong, that's only because it errs on the side of charity and understatement. The enormity of the mistakes of Monte Cassino was misunderstood and overlooked then—remains under-reported and under-understood still now, these seventy-odd years after—basically because Monte Cassino was never an experience to be explained by black ink on white paper in hometown newspapers or in *The New York Times*, or by age-smeared kinescopes with Ed Herlihy doing the voice-over, but rather an event that can only be appreciated—if that's the word—when it's been mud-splattered together in shades of grays and red.

The gray would be the hue created by that dirty smudge between this story's heroes and its villains, its Stars'n'Stripers and its Swastikas. Equal shares of nobility and sacrifice, foolishness and hubris, residing in grandiose splendor on both sides. Look at the old pictures, watch the old movies—all of them shades of gray and fading fast.

The red that leaks across this event—smearing the truth as it flows—came from the blood of three hundred and fifty thousand men. That is too many pints of plasma to be written off as wartime necessity. A lot of wives and kids left lonely on Christmas morning, this year and the next, and the next, and the next. Papa, he ain't never coming home—died Over There, died in the War. Visits by sad-faced officers and pasty-faced chaplains, clutching folded flags and rosary beads, walking sheepishly up to the front door of the clapboard houses filled with people who knew what was coming the moment they saw that khaki Ford staff car pull up out front and park. "Please, God, don't let them stop here, let them park down the street a little, one block over, anywhere's else but here. The Gallagars have a boy over there. Make it their son instead, please. Make it somebody else's soldier, not mine."

Also: priceless and irreplaceable art treasures were destroyed for no better reason than incompetence and impatience. Culture crushed by crud.

But numbers and names are simply numbers and names. Voices mean a lot more.

The voices in this book are small attempts to explain what happened during that historically bitter Italian winter, but the truth is—even with voices—this book is little more than a thin shadow of the event. A shadow is an outline traced by the lack of light, an area demanding to be further illuminated. And to become further illuminated, the reader should read a fact-heavy and full-throated work called *Monte Cassino: The Hardest Fought Battle of World War II,* by a guy named Mathew Parker, an Englishman. Then put that one down and pick up *Monte Cassino: The Story of the Most Controversial Battle of World War II,* by a couple of Davids, Hapgood and Richardson. If your eyes still aren't too heavy or misty, and your mind isn't too misery-bloated by then, go take a peek at those videos of Monte Cassino—some from Twentieth Century Fox, or from the History War Channel, and those called

"The Soldiers' Story," or six parts of "The Battle for Monte Cassino." You can YouTube them all.

If this book is the rumor, or the screamer, then these other sources are the quiet facts. Voices dripping with misery, facts painted in shades of gray. The reader/viewer can put in the red.

You've already met my two loud-mouth pals, Mack and Scooter—no further names needed—these guys being fictional compilations of the thousands of American G.I.'s who fought and were destroyed, either totally or in part, either then or later and forever, by what happened over there, and is still happening today wherever snotty politicians are believing they are men with balls of steel simply because it's not their balls being crushed. With your permission, Mack and Scooter will be taking part in the discussion.

Mack was a high school dropout who joined the service on July 25, 1943, then served in the U.S. Fifth Army…

***

Mack: *Petoola's* Fifth Army, he'd insist.

***

…in *Petoola's* Fifth Army, 36th Division, southern Italy. Mustered out in 1946, Mack went on to become a copyboy, then a cub reporter, then a staff writer, then a blue collar "dems and doz" columnist for *The Brooklyn Eagle*—where he kept looking for mittens or hats that Walt Whitman might have left hanging around the office in one of the desk drawers or coat closets.

Scooter left college in Utah to eventually join the 36th in Italy and—against all odds, geographic and cultural—became

Mack's best buddy. And against even *greater* odds, they both survived Southern Italy. Limbs intact. Psyches maybe not so much.

After the war Scooter latched onto a G.I. loan and somehow snagged a Budweiser distributorship in Utah—probably because no one else figured it had any chance—and he then went on to become one of those successful businessmen who somehow manage to keep the accent on the "man" instead of on the "business." This guy Scooter—as was often pointed out around Salt Lake—could sell beer to a Mormon.

And did.

***

Scooter: Yes, I did. Still do.

***

The 36th had been known as the Texas Division, but...

***

Mack: We're neither one of us from Texas.

***

"That's right, you're not from Texas, that's right, you're not from Texas, that's right, you're not from Texas, but Texas loves you anyhow." You guys know that one? Lyle Lovett?

***

Mack and Scooter: What?

***

Never mind. Was after your time. What happened was— so many good young Texas boys were either de-limbed or made defunct by the earlier battles—prior to and again during the bloody *Rapido* River crossing…

***

Mack: *Attempted* crossing.

***

Attempted crossing…

***

Mack: The whole stinking mess brain-child-ed, of course, by Petoola.

***

…by Petoola…

***

Mack: Twice.

***

Twice. So many of the Texas boys were deemed inoperable—for battle or for life—either by enemy fire, friendly fire, or self-inflicted "I gotta get outta here" fire—that the 36th was replenished by doe-eyed young red-asses like Mack and Scooter, sent up to the front to fill the bloody boots of those who were gone. There to serve honorably and well, upholding the glory of the Texas 36th, hailing from far away places like Utah and Brooklyn, but now doing their work in sunny, bloody Italy.

These two best buddies, parted by mustering out and by Military-Geographic Separation, post V-E Day, were to sit down together in a Queens, New York, bar with smoke-smeared windows and grease-smeared tables, years later, the 1980s, years removed from the event that had scarred and scared them both forever, so really not removed from it at all. They were to discuss the event as best they could. As best as their emotions and memories and macho self-image and scar tissue would allow.

Mack brought along his honesty and his brass bazooka attitude and his army-issue curse words.

Scooter brought the sensitivity and bought the rounds of beer. Bud, of course.

***

Mack: He somehow gets it for free or something. Or else half-off. Company brew.

***

Their dialogues here are all fictitious; but what they have to say about Monte Cassino is the truth, and so they have been allowed to jump time and to jump in, onto the pages of this book.

***

Scooter: Was Churchill…

Mack: That's right, that god-damn limey was the one got us down there in the first place. Him and all his "Soft Underbelly" bullshit. What a load of crap that was.

Scooter: Well, Roosevelt, he…

Mack: Convinced Roosevelt not to rely on D-Day, on Normandy.

Scooter: Was known as "Operation Overlord" back then.

Mack: What are you, Intelligence? Yeah, Churchy was the overlord all right. Fat Stogie-breath says to the cripple, "We're just not ready for that yet, guv'nor. Not enough boats. Troops too green." That's where we should've been all along, getting ready for *that* push.

Scooter: Well, Churchill was worried, figured his people couldn't take another brush-off. Off the continent again. They—his folks, his troops—they'd already suffered through France's falling, and Dunkirk, down in the Balkans—so Churchy knew they couldn't take another one of those hits.

Mack: Another ass-kicking.

Scooter: Something like that could kill off that old limey confidence for good.

Mack: Didn't want the war in his own back yard, that's all. Out on his front lawn, tramping down his pretty, Brit-y daisies. Let the I-tals have it instead. Let them play host to the party, they asked for it.

***

That heavy-set gentleman—with those British fat rolls under his chin and British beef in his belly, Cuban cigar residue and tobacco lint mixing in his mouth—had met with Roosevelt and the Allies in early 1943 in Casablanca. By then the place had been liberated, Humphrey "Rick" Bogart having walked off into the fog beside his new best buddy, Claude Rains, with Rick humming a Dooley Wilson piano solo and trying to forget how damned-good Ingrid Bergman had looked in Paris—just so naked and waiting for it. He'd always have that.

But, as Stogie-breath reached across the table for another helping of his kidney pie and brandy, George Marshall was whispering into FDR's good right ear, "We're Americans, sir, Ulysses S. Grant *Americanos.* We know the shortest distance between two points, don't we? How'd we get the country expanded all the way out to the West Coast, if I might ask, Mr. President, sir, huh? A straight line, wasn't it? Yes sir, some Indians and some scruples stood in our way back then, but that's the way we went, straight ahead, that's the way we got there. A straight line, drawn across a map with a yardstick and a trail of blood. And so that's how we get to Berlin too. Don't you think? A three-point stance on top the Cliffs of Dover, like a good running back—a Red Grange—Hike! we crash into the line, head down, legs churning—nothing hurts till later—keep the legs pumping, the knees bending, all the way to the Reich's goal-line, with maybe Bronko Nagurski or Forest Evashevski running the interference, providing the blocking. What do you say, sir? Don't you think?"

By the way, don't take any of these quotes to the bank, or try using them at a panel discussion of military war writers; all they are is just a bitter old tour-guide's figuring of what was said. So FDR nodded, thought about it, sucked on his cigarette holder, thought some more, maybe went home and ran it by Eleanor after a quick lubing of his secretary, but still couldn't decide. Thinking: "Look, Winston's probably right, we're not ready to cross the Channel yet, but we gotta show Uncle Joe we're here for the fight, we're not just working the corner as his cut-man. We have to do something *now*. So we can say to the Steel Man, 'Look, Joe, our troops are chasing Rommel all over North Africa, we mean business.' After all, we sure don't need any one-sided peace talks—you and Adolph—at this point. All we have to fear is fear itself, and of course getting some of our boys killed down there."

When FDR told that to Marshall, Marshall just shrugged. Went off to bed.

It took ten days of jawing at Casablanca, but finally the U.S. of A.—a bit fuzzy-headed and hoodwinked maybe, or at least self-delusional—caved in and went south. And so it came to be that somehow Old Stogie-breath convinced them all: Tunis it was, Sicily it would be, *Napoli*, soon to be Rome and up and up and up. Rolling north as fast as tanks and half-tracks could accelerate, pedal to the metal, foot to the floorboard.

FDR, feeling pretty good now, telling Uncle Joe: Look, we'll be in Rome in a couple weeks. Both of them, Britain too, already knowing they'd win this war, eventually, after killing enough troops on both sides, and then they'd get to divvy up Europe afterwards. Everybody angling for a piece of that Post War Pie.

***

Mack: So old Churchy, he figured we'd make a good distraction down there puncturing the Soft Underbelly while things got put together for the real show up in Normandy.
Scooter: Is that what we were down there? A distraction?
Mack: I presume so. I guess that's all we were.
Scooter: A diversion. Like a magician's trick.

Mack: Didn't feel like magic. At the time.

***

So the Yanks and the Brits—each keeping a wary watch on each other out of the corner of one eye, as they beaded down on Jerry with their M-1's and Brent guns with the other—got their shoes sandy in the Sahara, then hit the beaches at Sicily, then hopped and slogged their way onto the main land, the toe of the boot, ankle high and risin', like a good-sized flood of Mediterranean deep blue sea water.

Monte—Churchy's fair-haired boy, his Golden Childe—had planned ahead and had managed to hit the beach with camera crews directly in front of him—photogs shooting footage while walking backwards—and with crates of cigarettes for his boys being toted ashore in the background of the shot. Petoola—he stands there in the shadows, watching, jealous, furious, getting no ink at all in all this—and he vows to never let *that* shit happen again. Not if *he* can help it, and turns out he can.

Meanwhile, kids are dying on the beach and upland too. Off camera, of course.

Afterwards, twenty-six hundred Allied vessels get hosed off, dried up, patched and puttied and painted, and sailed up to Britain's east coast, now officially pre-owned-vessels, but with low mileage, only been used once, to smack the Axis in the Med.

Some of those Med landings went pretty well, even better than predicted, with every G.I. Division being assured beforehand, "Oh, no, you guys won't be the first wave in. You're scheduled to be third, maybe fourth wave, tops. Shit'll all be cleared by the time you guys get there. It'll be warm water, ankle deep, then chilled wine and warm women. It'll be nice, you'll like it. Maybe even get your picture in the paper."

That invasion, that beach landing, could have been worse, and it often was. It was a lot worse for the paratroopers, the guys who were mostly getting killed by "friendly fire," which doesn't feel so friendly when it's your own legs being blown off.

And it had gotten even worse than that, for everybody, when Rommell began blasting his way back at the Kasserine Pass, then smirked and called the Yanks "green and young"—which they were, but they toughened up quick—combat does that—and finally the good guys could sit awhile on the warm Italian dirt, prop a helmet on a knee, and begin envisioning a fairly easy sojourn north to all that cool wine and warm women, accompanied by honor and horniness and a thousand mean-growling Sherman tanks.

Let's head on up to Rome, baby.

***

But tanks and armored vehicles quickly proved themselves to be useless for the drive up Route 6, that cool afternoon motor trip to *Bella Roma*.

***

Mack: You know what I think? If "Old Blood and Guts" had been in charge, you think they would've mucked up Cassino the way they did?

Scooter: First, he didn't get that name from his *own* blood, his *own* guts. Was ours, the enlisted man's B'n'G.

Mack: Still, if'n "Old B and G" had been running things…

Scooter: Two things, three things—first, he *wasn't* in charge any more…

Mack: Fucken Petoola.

Scooter: That's right, Petoola was our man.

Mack: What a fucken mistake that was.

Scooter: Patton was no longer the man calling shots, except maybe calling for shots of booze. He having made the mistake of slapping, punching, maybe quick pistol-whipping some poor kid who'd had enough, was sitting on the side of a white-sheeted hospital bed, making the mistake of not bleeding on the outside and of still having all four of his limbs. How many guys, our age, younger, we'd seen—all busted up inside—like that?

Mack: A lot.

Scooter: Lots. Eternal internal bleeding, right? You and me included, at times, right? You've seen me that way, I've seen you that way, right?

Mack: Yeah. We have.

Scooter: We weren't cowards, were we? We weren't jellyfish.

Mack: Nope. We were mules is all we were.

Scooter: We were soldiers, that's all. Ups and down. Down and out, revelry, up and at 'em. So was this poor kid. So Patton makes the mistake—not just of slapping the kid around, calling his a faggot—but making the mistake of doing it with the reporters present, present and writing, present and taking notes.

Mack: How'd they ever let that story get out anyway? You'd think they would've killed it, could've easy.

Scooter: Amazing. I don't know. Maybe somebody didn't like him. But, the result being—Patton was not our beloved leader at the time. It was Petoola.

Mack: Shit-eating grin, only too glad to take over. *That* asshole.

Scooter: But my second point, even if he were still around—George P. that is—he was a tank man, and tanks, they were mostly useless, remember? Between the valleys, the mountains, the artillery craters, the rivers, the flooding, the muck, the rain, all the problems they had with the Bailey Bridges, you could not use those Shermans.

Mack: Yup. Twentieth Century, modern world, and we're fighting not using tanks, instead we're using…

***

Mules.

Smart money around the Pentagon had been predicting this one would be the first of the modern wars. Having been predicted at the ass end of the First World War: Air Power and Mechanization, that's the way to go, that'd be the way it would be from now on. Slit trenches? Bayonets? Hand-to-hand, man-to-man charges and counter-charges, a hundred fifty yards here, two hundred yards there, back and forth, back and forth? No, never. That was soooo World War I. This one would be won by factories producing V-8 engines and jet turbines and Liberty Ships and troop carriers and tanks with metal tracks the size of billboards, all growling and grunting and moving forward with aplomb.

But it did not turn out that way.

Turned out instead, it was mules.

A couple hard-working, sure-footed, no-questions-asking mules were worth a brigade of tanks. You'd have a hard time looking up the number of mules killed over there back then—falling off cliffs, blown to bits by mines below and artillery above, starved to death. Eaten. Eaten—diseased but still tasty—eaten alive, to stay alive, ward off starvation. No numbers kept.

In some cruel eyes, through high-powered field glasses, from the safety of miles behind the front line, the fighting men were little more than mules themselves. You wouldn't find the career men making that statement in *Stars and Stripes*, but Command actions lent credence to that notion. Both men and mules made to slog through stupidity on their way to…everybody was hoping…to a world of less torture and fewer killings. Meanwhile, Allied air attacks were destroying towns, livestock, women, children and Allied soldiers. Setting the precedence for things to come at Monte Cassino.

***

Well, it didn't take long for the Italians to get sick of this stuff, and they officially bailed out of the war at that point. *Basta, basta.* In a way, that was too bad. If it had been the Italian foot soldiers defending the Monastery at Monte Cassino, things would have gone a lot easier for guys like Mack and Scooter. The Monastery probably would still be standing. The original one.

***

Mack: We would've been suffering from heartburn and syphilis instead of shrapnel and gangrene.

***

Hitler quickly delivered a nice-size chunk of his army—battle-hardened by the Russian Front—including his toughest paratroopers, those psychotics looking for a place to play—to replace the Italians, most of whom had decided to walk home. The *paisans'* feet were bloodied, bandaged, swollen, rotted and hurting, but they were singing and laughing all the way anyway. Going home.

Mussolini was put under house arrest *(*"Hey, c'mon, you guys know me, I'm the guy who got the trains running on time"), but when a small group of SS commandoes flew in on a German glider and pointed their rifle muzzles at the guards, demanding *Il Duce's* release, the startled key-keepers all said, "Hey, no trouble here, you want him, he's yours, we don't want him. What are we gonna do with him anyway? He eats too much, complains too much, brags too much, and his fat jowls would make a lousy looking trophy on the living room wall."

But Benito just couldn't keep out of trouble and what the Italians eventually *did* do with him was hang him by his heals in the town square. Turns out his jowls looked a little bit better as a trophy when hanging upside-down.

Up until that time, Mussolini had to have been one of the most self-deluded leaders in history (You think *that's* an easy list to get placed high on?)—believing as he did: 1. the people they all love me; 2.my staff is loyal; 3. I got a lot of influence over this Hitler fella.

Self-delusions like these tend to leak out of your ears and nose and even through the top of your head when you're hanging up-side-down in the town square and little old *goo-mahs*—black hair buns, black moles, black mustaches, black dresses—are shoving and elbowing each other, trying to get a bit of your blood on their handkerchiefs as they're kicking you in the head and the balls, if they can reach their spindly old Italian legs up that high.

***

Monte Cassino. You get all sorts of statistics on how many good people were eradicated down there that winter. Low-ball: Germans twenty-five thousand, Allies fifty-four thousand. High-ball could go as high as…

***

Mack: I could use a high-ball long about now, even more back then.
Scooter: My Bud's no good, not good enough?
Mack: It's very good, very fine beer. Very free.
Scooter: Thank you.

***

High-ball: eighty thousand on one side, a hundred and five thousand on the other. Some say even that's too low. Noncombatants? *Gli Sfortunati?* No way to tell, really. They were just mules, just some more mules to use, cruise and lose. No stats kept. So let's just say, all together, three hundred and fifty thousand human casualties. Written out in numeral numbers, it looks like this: 350,000.

    Americans killed in Viet Nam: 58,236

    Deaths from terrorists attacks, September 11, 2001: 2,819

    Population of Tampa, Florida: 340,882

    Three hundred and fifty thousand.

    Calling Monte Cassino "Five Months of Insanity" is putting a positive spin on it, polishing up the image. It was worse than that. One battle in southern Italy that few people remember or care about.

    350,000.

    And that, my friend, is just the beginning.

    Let me take you back to before the beginning. How it all started. Believe it or not, this story begins amid purity and sanctity, in piety and in grandeur.

    ***

Chapter Two:
The Life of St. Benedict and the History of His Abbey

"For, more than thirteen centuries ago,
Benedict fleeing from the gates of Rome,
A youth disgusted with its vice and woe,
Sought in these mountain solitudes a home.
He founded here his Convent and his Rule,
Of prayer and work, and counted work as prayer,
The pen becomes a clarion, and his school
Flames like a beacon in the midnight air."

-from "Monte Cassino" by Henry Wadsworth Longfellow 1875

***

Contents included, the Monastery at Monte Cassino had to be considered among the most inspirational edifices—among the most the most inspirational *things*—ever created by the hand of man; and certainly it nears the top of the list of the most inspirational things ever wantonly destroyed by that hand.

Not too many years after Pontius Pilate's demolition-construction crew had finished cleaning up the mess left over from the Resurrection (busted granite chunks and sepulcher rock all over the place—mud, stone, angel dust…) Saint Benedict was born, 480 A.D., in Nursia, a small town nestled near the slightly less-small town of Spoleta, seventy-eight miles north of the big town, Rome.

The baby did not exhibit many saintly qualities right off, and he didn't appear to have any grandiose life plans; he quickly grew into a young man who simply wanted to be a holy hermit. His ambition was to live a life of quiet and pious solitude, thinking about God and heaven, surviving on a couple mouthfuls of Adriatic fish and well water, keeping the mouth clear for all that praying and chanting.

His family was of upper crust Nursian society, and the folks weren't crazy about the idea of their boy pursuing God rather than greenbacks, but—kids these days, what can you do—they let him walk his own life's path. Mama and Papa were even less pleased when Benedict set up housekeeping in a cave, a little chunked-out piece of rock in the area of Subiaco, fifty miles outside of Rome—but it could have been a million miles, the ambiance was so opposed to the "vice and woe" of the big *città*. Except for the absence of steel plate reinforcement and machinegun emplacements, Benedict's little pill box home was not that different from the stalls that German engineers would dig and decorate fifteen centuries later, not far from here.

Benedict pointed out to his folks that it was a very nice cave, had everything he needed, with few worldly distractions, and you could see heaven, or at least heaven's floor—the sky—by hanging your head out the entrance. The folks just shrugged, looked at each other and shook their heads. They loved their boy.

But alas, young Benedict's plans for a life of quiet solitude and religious dedication were not to be. His mistake was being a little bit *too* pious, a little *too* other-worldly—he got himself a fare amount of street cred that way—and then on top of that he began pulling off a couple lower grade miracles in the name of Our Savior, Jesus Christ. Nothing flashy—more water-to-wine and curing-some-rheumatiz kind of stuff than popping dead folks up from the dead—but still, soon many of the kids in the surrounding neighborhoods were bugging him to let them follow him down the path to sanctity and to salvation and to his cave.

Once a posse has been formed, and you've got yourself an entourage walking so close behind you that they're stepping on the backs of your sandals whenever you try walking the Stations of the Cross or just heading down to the vineyards for some grapes, it becomes nearly impossible to remain a practicing hermit. "Go play somewhere else," Benedict would tell the group—a group that had now swelled into a crowd and was pressed up against all three walls of his cave. Just blessing yourself in that cramped space could put somebody's eye out in you weren't careful.

"We're not just hangers-on," they tried explaining to the future saint. "We're not leeches, bloodsuckers. What we are is…we're Disciples."

"Of who?"

"Of you. Honest."

"Jesus."

So in 528 (a number which doesn't even look like a year until you slap that A.D. on its end), Benedict took the gang to Montecassino (Montecassino apparently being all one word back then, the artillery and bombs not having busted it into pieces quite yet), and the next year he and the crew built the original Monastery there. He chose a spot on the highest point of the Montecassino Massif, above a web of rivers with lovely names like *Rapido*, *Garigliano*, and *Liri*.

A massif is a ridge line, an elevated series of lesser peaks leading to the highest one. The foot soldiers of the winter of '43-'44, on both sides, would get to know this area well: every gulch, every gap, every pile of rock, every elevation, every chunk of dirt.

Centuries before Benedict, the holy Romans had used the same spot to build themselves a temple to Apollo. From there the A-list god could fight off the hordes of devils that were living in woods where the "mad multitude of infidels did offer most wicked sacrifice." It wouldn't be surprising if some of those sacrifices victimized mules—just as the poor, hardworking beasts were to be sacrificed fifteen centuries later by guys wearing medals and epaulets instead of togas and laurel wreaths. In wars and in religious clashes, God always seems to be on both sides; at least that's what each side says He is. He Himself usually isn't talking.

Benedict was thinking of this place, this palace of his, as being a fortress against the forces of Lucifer, never once considering the influx of drunken Poles and wild Gurkhas that was to come. And fortress-like it was, a squat monolith of solid stone set fifteen hundred feet above the *Liri* plains, looking over the *Via Casilina* (now Route 6), which the Romans had built ten centuries earlier as the best way to get from southern Italy up into Rome. As we'll see, this Via, this super-strategic Route 6, remained for centuries the choice route north from here to there.

***

Mack: (Singing) If you ever plan to motor north/ Just take my way, that's the highway…?
Scooter: To go forth?
Mack: Maybe.

***

There was a good reason that the emperors decided that "All roads lead to Rome." If you're running an empire, and you don't want hordes of oppressed peasants getting together for a mutiny, what you do, you build good roads fanning out from the hub of things, so that your troops can get there quickly to quell any monkey business, while at the same time you keep the roads running laterally in bad shape, so that mutinies can't spread horizontally. They did some real thinking, those Romans, when they weren't busy lining up to use the vomitoriums.

***

Scooter: And, as always, the idea is to not give the common folk any kind of break whatsoever.

***

So Benedict built his Monastery to look more like a fortress than a church. Remember how in Ayn Rand's book, *The Fountainhead*, the great secular architect Howard Roark (or Gary Cooper, if you just saw the movie) ticks everybody off because the great church he designs has no spires and towers that lift up the spirit and eyes toward the heavens, but instead keeps things squat and solid and low to the ground? Why aspire to the heavens, Howard would be asking/saying, let's stay concerned with keeping grounded. Well, *Abbazia di Montecassino*, especially in its later incarnations, took on that same earthbound, here-to-stay look. Critics would say "Squat," the monks would call it, "Sensible."

And Benedict was to remain there at his beloved Monastery for the rest of his life. "Why would I ever want to move from this little chunk of heaven we got here? I should want to go back to living in a cave?"

His sister Scholastica, who would go on to gain the saintly aura of her brother if not the fame, joined him there.

Benedict told his Disciples that if they were going to stick around, there were going to be some rules, some *Rules*, so he wrote down what became the *Rule of St. Benedict*—spelling out in flowery longhand exactly what it takes to live the life of a monk. The *Rule* became the guide book for monastic life everywhere in medieval Europe. It still stands today as the way things should be done. Pray, eat, sleep, don't turn away strangers, keep a clean nose, know which way the wind blows.

Benedict had wanted to add a statute forbidding the consumption of wine, but these being Italians he was dealing with—and with wine always being close at hand for ceremonial purposes—he let that one slide. Too tough to enforce. So the monks could enjoy a nice *Frascati* with their meals—a beverage that everyone approved of and would continue to be imbibed and enjoyed well into the Twentieth Century, by aficionados who didn't have God on their mind and who had more than simple bread products on their plate.

Mythology tells up that upon completion of his dream house, Benedict took a step back and quietly predicted, "This house will be destroyed four times. And then rebuilt four times."

The monks, who weren't supposed to talk too much, felt they just had to blurt out, "You're shitting us, really? Four times?"

Benedict vigorously insisted. "It is true. Destroyed four times, only to be rebuilt four times."

A monk who had given up the treasures of the world but had held onto his wise guy attitude, responded, "Well, we figured it had to keep getting rebuilt the first three times so it could get destroyed again, but still, after all our work, this is really depressing."

Benedict died and was buried there at the Monastery, buried next to his sister, the previously mentioned and equally canonized but not as well named Saint Scholastica.

Soon after St. Benedict's passing, a marauding horde of Lombards—looking and acting something like John Belushi in "Animal House"—sacked and destroyed the building for no other reason than that is what they were paid to do.

Pope Gregory II commissioned an architectural genius named Brescian Petronace to rebuild the place, which Brescian gladly did. As always is the case with state-run building projects, the reconstruction cost more and took longer than Brescian's estimate, but was eventually completed and those keeping score notched a single line on the big scorecard and said, "Uh-oh, looking good, Brescian, but that's just One, and the Old Man told us Four."

By this time the Monastery, this Abbey at Monte Cassino, was regarded as the European fountainhead of monastic life. From its walls it breathed out piety and spiritual strength across the Mediterranean and across the entire Continent. In exchange, it took in the greatest artwork and scholarship that the Christian world had to offer. It became no less than the major depository of the artistic wealth of the Christian religion.

In the basilica a group of monks might be warbling their Gregorian Chant while in the *collegia* a group of their brothers might be transcribing ageless manuscripts, working into the night with quill pens and cramping fingers. "Offer it up, you're scribbling for God."

Then the Saracens, another Belushi-like band, decided that they could not let that stand, so in 883 they not only pulverized the place once again, but this time burned it too, setting fire to the rubble so that the holy place would be destroyed once and for all. For good measure they killed St. Bertarius, who was running the place at the time. A few monks managed to escape (much as they would again in World War II), then to return and rebuild from the rubble once again.

Benedictine scholars chalked a big number "2" on the scoreboard and waited.

By now the Popes knew they had something special on this hill tucked in beneath the Abruzzi Mountains, and so they continued to pack the cells and rooms and basilica with: priceless man-scrawled manuscripts of faith; mosaics and enamels unrivaled anywhere else in the world; golden chalices used to hold the body blood of Christ; other precious objects of liturgy and clergy; and artwork which could show Western Culture what Western Culture was. Hadn't they been paying attention to Benedict's prediction?

Okay, you saw this coming—in 1349 an earthquake reduced the place to nothing but a few crumbling walls. By now even the Phoenix or Rocky Balboa would have tossed in the towel, but people with God on their side are a stubborn lot, and once again the walls of the Monastery rose from the ashes. This place was harder to kill than a furniture store that keeps flashing, "Going Out of Business—Big Sale to End Soon" signs in its front window.

The Abbey was nearly destroyed again in 1504, during a French and Spanish war, but the destruction was halted when the Spaniard in charge was hit by a dream-vision that told him, "Hands off." This was a blessed event, but it had its down side too, because that destruction would have upped the number for Benedict's prediction to the requisite four, and maybe would have curtailed the air attack of Flying Fortresses in '44.

Each demolition, and every recreation, made the place stronger, more holy, more eternal, if anything ever can get *more* eternal.

***

Picture the place as it was in 1944 like this: If the Pentagon were plopped down on the top of a mountain, with nothing else around but grass and granite and some scrubby olive bushes. That Arlington VA monstrosity was built with earthly rather than celestial things in mind; low-down, tough, solid, immovable, taking no crap from anyone. You've seen those aerial shots of the Pentagon—you see a massive, low-slung, tough-looking piece of hard rock that you just know is going nowhere and keeping secrets.

Now reduce the five sides of the Pentagon to four, and you've got a picture of Benedict's Abbey as it was structured for hundreds of years before World War II and then again, rebuilt, for all these years since. Remember to place that image on top of a mountain with nothing else manmade in sight, and you've got the picture.

Five court yards, an immense basilica, a school for local children, a seminary for aspiring priests, bell towers, statues, maze after maze of cells and altars, walls twenty (I said *twenty*) foot wide at the base and fifty feet high. With only one way in or out, and that entrance secured by a pair of bronze doors that were legendary and impenetrable.

The windows looked like darkened eyes, hundreds of square eyes, with every one of them looking *down*, down at the valley and plains below, looking for devils, for intruders, for threats that could come creeping up the steep and rocky mountainside in attack. Could be the devil, could be drunken Poles, but either way, the building kept watch.

For centuries the Abbey remained a working Monastery, an anchor-site of Christianity, the target for pilgrimages from around the world, a safe haven for the dispossessed and the needy, the storehouse of art treasures that were unrivaled anywhere, and the wealthiest monastery in the world.

In its peak years in the 1600s, the place was getting over eighty thousand visitors per annum, a sort of medieval Disneyland with Benedict and the Many Monks instead of Snow White and the Seven Dwarfs. Like Walt's place, the Monastery sat atop an equally expansive parallel world just below ground level. A mirror image basement, a cellar to prepare meals, to stow roots and fruits and cleaning equipment, a place to get away from the tourists and pilgrims. And from the explosives.

14 Feb 44: The sound of the monks' Gregorian Chant was to be drowned out by the hum of aircraft on the horizon—mean, getting louder, getting closer. Afterwards, the aircraft bomb bay would be lighter by thousands of tons, and the sound of the engines would be growing quiet. And the Monastery would be no more.

***

Fourteen hundred years of piety, culture, art and civilization. Architecture. A treasure-packed study in eternal indestructibility. It would take the B-17 Flying Fortresses but a few hours to turn the place into mush.

***

Chapter Three:
Jerry Builds a Meat Grinder

"Well I remember the low arch and dark,
The courtyard with its well, the terrace wide,
From which, far down, the valley like a park,
Veiled in the evening mists, was dim decried.
The day was dying, and with feeble hands
Caressed the mountain-tops; the vales between
Darkened; the river in the meadow-lands
Sheathed itself as a sword, and was not seen."

-from "Monte Cassino" by Henry Wadsworth Longfellow 1875

***

Unlike most of its middle-aged women, Italy is a skinny country, especially its central and southern parts—the *Mezzogiorno,* south of the noonday sun—where dry land runs barely seventy-five miles from shining Tyrrhenian to shining Adriatic Sea. For some purposes you can cut that distance in half, since the Apennine mountain range runs the length of the country, effectively bisecting the boot, running down from Switzerland to Sicily like a giant metaphor-mixing backbone. At the very heart of the vertebra rests Rome, the Allies' target in 1943, lying on the thin western slice of that body cavity.

The Allied forces had successfully hopped across the Mediterranean from North Africa onto that sunny soccer ball at the toe of Italy's boot called Sicily, and from there onto the mainland itself. Allied commanders to a man were feeling pretty good; they were yet to realize that this game had barely begun.

That west-side corridor that they had to battle their way up through is crisscrossed with rugged, lateral running mountains and ragged cliffs, as well as rivers that twist back and forth so many times that one Allied general's driver finally took his exasperated hands off the Jeep's steering wheel and complained, "Every fucken river in this country is named the *Volturo*."

The Good Guys managed to battle their way up to *Napoli* and then some, up to the area where the Abruzzi Mountains turned jagged, steep, and potentially more deadly. The rivers there are sloppy, meandering, and each one can act as a drowner of tanks. The battle thus far had been a blindside creep through a labyrinthine maze, where around every corner sat a German soldier with a Spandau machinegun, a pile of stick grenades, and a smug look on his Super Race face.

Only four Italian roads heading north in this Lazio Region were solid enough to handle the tanks and heavy equipment that the Allies were depending on. Two of those roads ran east of the mountains, territory controlled by Montgomery's troops and offering no benefit to those who had their eye on Rome. Even if your troops on that side of the country were able to push the Germans back north, you'd still have to get across the mountains in order to get over to the city.

So a western road it would have to be; there were two to choose from. Route 7, the old Roman *Via Appia*, ran along the coast and was pressed by the Tyrrhenian Sea on the left, the mountains on the right. It was a route that could be easily flooded from one side, smashed by rock slides from the other. Too dangerous.

And so the strategy had shriveled down from "All roads lead to Rome" to "General, there's only one way to get there from here," and that one way was Route 6, the old Roman *Via Casilina.*

Over on the other team, some level-headed German leaders thought that their best strategy would be to fall back to northern Italy—make their Custer's stand up there by the Alps—but some un-level heads like Hitler's were too proud to accept that idea, and Hitler's was the only head that counted, level or not. So the Krauts of the South would stand (and kneel and lie) and make their fight right there.

Everybody knew that if the Allies could push forward its troops and equipment—and push the Germans back through the *Liri* Valley, then the route to Rome itself—with all of its political, military and propaganda values—would be ripe for the bite and ready for the pickin'.

You didn't have to finish in the top half of your class at West Point to figure all this out. Petoola and Eisenhower and Montgomery and Marshall all know it. And on the German side, bright guys like Smiling Al Kesselring and Frido vonSenger knew it too.

Yup, control the *Liri* Valley and you control the route to Pope-land. The Valley was actually the juncture of *two* valleys, where the *Liri* joined the *Rapido.* The trouble was this: At the head of that valley juncture stood an imposing seventeen hundred foot-high hill. And at the top of that hill stood a building from which your enemy could watch you, bombard you, fire down on you, control you, put your troops through a meat grinder like the world had never before seen, stop you dead—dead—dead—and then more dead, in your tracks.

The building was the Monastery at Monte Cassino.

***

For any army of foot soldiers to get control of that chunk of land, it would have to fight its gruesome way up and across the Cassino Massif, that ridgeline of granite and crevice strung like rosary beads across the sky and ending with the Crucifix itself—the Monastery. The various beads on this rosary did not go by names like "Our Father" or "Hail Mary" or "Glory Be," but rather carried more prosaic titles like "Hill 593" or "Point 569." Over the course of the next hard winter, the press boys and the dog faces would give these black beads names like "The Mad Mile" and "Million Dollar Hill" (because somebody in Finance had figured out it was costing $25,000 to kill each German soldier. Ernie Pile suggested at that rate we could just buy them off).

The high ground lying before the Monastery took on the name of "Snake's Head Ridge" (also called "Snakehead"). Both names are fitting, especially if the snake was a cobra—coiled and ready to strike.

On this tract of land—land that previously had been desired by nobody but the monks and the local peasants—the Germans set about building a defensive line that could only be penetrated by an army willing to destroy itself.

***

The war was over; that was the sad part. No one on either side was mouthing those words, no one issued the press releases, but by late 1943, all that was to come would be pointless. The Third Reich was swirling down the toilet bowl without a chance in its self-made hell of reversing the flow. Their North Atlantic U-Boat campaign had been neutralized, and despite Rommel's brilliance North Africa had been lost, and Operation Overlord would soon be landing troops at Normandy to begin pushing east, and… and… and, there had been… Stalingrad. The Battle of Stalingrad had been fought the winter before, and that body-shot had taken the wind and much of the life out of the Reich—it should have led to their corner men tossing in the bloody towel, but what can you do when you've got a madman working your corner and calling the shots. You answer the bell, you keep on bleeding and sucking on your mouthpiece, and you hope to be carried from the ring with a usable piece of your brain still intact.

The problem for the advancing Allies was: the Russians had taught the Germans a lesson or two at Stalingrad, and the Germans had learned some things well. The Russians had taught Napoleon the same lesson in the century before, but at least the French had accepted it, packed up their notebooks and pencils and guns and gone home to make love and cook entrées with heavy cream sauces. The Krauts instead had said, "Hey, so *that's* how you fight a defensive war. Heck, we can do that."

So really, the Germans had learned only one of the two main lessons to be learned. Lesson One was that the war was over, that the Nazis were doomed—but that one didn't really take root in Arian minds until a few years later, when the Allis were pushing across Europe trying to beat the Ruskies into Berlin.

The Germans had only learned Lesson Number Two during their Stalingrad winter, but they had learned it very well and very deeply; that lesson being the one about how to play defense. How hunkering down and fighting to protect each inch of territory can take a lot out of an advancing army, until the advance itself becomes a piece of hot shrapnel in the gut of the invaders.

During its back-peddling to Stalingrad, the Russian army had three things going for it: a huge country that forced the advancing Germans to extend supply lines to untenable lengths; a rugged and toxic countryside made more rugged and more toxic by the Scorched Earth policy; and the Russian winter.

In southern Italy a year later, the now-defensive minded Germans had: a skinny country that would easily predict the advancing army's route; a maze of rugged mountains and cliffs that allowed the defenders to set up their observation points and artillery sights on the High Ground (it was always easier to shoot and look down rather than up); and a winter, while not to be compared to that winter of Stalingrad '42-'43—nothing could—was far from being the "Sunny Italy" of the postcards and the love ballads. It was to be the worst winter in Italy in memory, and that's taking nothing but the weather into consideration.

***

And so the Germans began work on preparations for the arrival of their cigar-smoking, often-whoring, rarely-caring, visitors.

First, they needed a name. They would not call the defensive link running nearly from sea to sea "Hands Across Italy," but rather "The Gustav Line."

The Germans chose a genius engineer to build the Line, and an even smarter guy to run it once it was built.

***

The engineer was General Hans Bessel, who came to the table packing a few valuable convictions:

One. Despite what the smart money was saying about this war being the first of the "scientific" wars—to be won and fought by the mechanization and automation of Twentieth Century science—it would really be a war to be won or lost in the old fashioned way: the way wars had been won and lost in the rat-infested trenches of the First World War; in the hand-to-hand combat-bloodied turrets of medieval castles, and in the caves of Pre-History. That is: One guy killing another guy face-to-face and hand-to-hand while their leaders sat and ate lunch. The most mechanical thing about this war would be the machine-like look of death on the faces of dead soldier lying by the side of the road.

Two. Therefore the enemy, with its superior number of tanks, planes, men and ammunition (Hans figured he'd have about 10% to 20% of the bullets that the other guys had) could be reduced to at best (for them) a stalemate, reduced by the installation and clever manning of an impregnable defensive fortification.

Of course in addition it would take thousands and thousands of brave, loyal and fanatical troops who would never come home from Italy, but Hans had a pocketful of those types.

So he set about building his Line. It could have been called the "Bessel" Line instead of the Gustav, but it wasn't.

First, realizing that the Allied army would prefer to travel on the horsepower of its tanks and armored vehicles instead of mule-power, the Germans blew up or otherwise destroyed the bridges over the network of meandering rivers.

Invading infantry would find fording the rivers to be nearly impossible. The river banks were generally steep, wide and muddy. The currents were often strong, the water was often cold. Hans had the land on each side of each river cleared away to barrenness, leaving no bushes or trees for attackers to hide behind.

Then the German engineers blew the dams on the *Rapido* (or *Gari*) and *Liri* Rivers, turning the valleys into impassible quagmires of mud and water.

All this put the heavy-moving, armored vehicles of the Allies out of play. In order to cross any of the rivers, it would become necessary for the Allies to construct Bailey Bridges, crude temporary structures that were little more than life-sized Erector Set pieces. And it's tough building with Erector Sets when you're being fired upon from above by bullets and rockets.

The rain, mud and muck had slowed the Allies' trip north as much as weaponry had, and that would be the case, even more so, from here on up.

The Germans also outfitted a series of underground caves and bunkers, some so sophisticated and strong that soldiers could sit and play a game of Doppelkopf, undisturbed by the Allied artillery shells raining down on the hillside around their nest. Some were even multi-room dwellings with phonographs, kitchens, couches—all the comforts of home. If the ghost of the young Saint Benedict was huddling ascetically in the corner of a cave reciting vespers, no one noticed.

The Germans on the hillsides had hundreds of bunkers and trenches and machinegun nests. A line of self-propelled automatic guns sat on the bluffs above the rivers. Often using a combination of foreign slave labor and fine German steel, Hans reinforced existing fissures with nearly indestructible plates and walls. Gun pits were blasted out of the mountainside rock. Entries to the caves and the pits were protected by iron doors that only allowed the protrusion of one object—the muzzle of a machinegun.

Pre-fab steel bunkers were brought in and deep-set into the mountainside. Pill boxes and dugouts were built to blend into the countryside, nearly invisible to aircraft or field glasses. Even some of the old farmhouses were reinforced with steel and weaponry and turned into dispersers of death and destruction.

Roads, fields, footpaths and riverbanks were pimpled with landmines—those insidious and incendiary devices that foot soldiers feared more than enemy gunfire. Taking a bullet to the shoulder or arm could almost be Hollywood heroic, or to the foot (self-inflicted or not) combat-ending, but losing legs and genitals to the landmines would do nothing to put a rosy glow on your arrival back home in the States.

Hans had buried over twenty-four thousand S-42 landmines just an inch or two below the fertile Italian soil and within the unforgiving Italian limestone and granite. The Yanks would begin calling the evil things "Bouncing Betties."

***

Scooter: Because that's what you did when your foot tapped one. You bounced.

***

To the Germans they were S-mines or "*Schümines*"…

***

Mack: Because they'd blow your shoes off.
Scooter: Worse.

***

Miles of barbed wire were strung across fields and river banks. Booby traps were set in any spot that looked like an unlikely spot for a booby trap. Railroad ties were used to block the already muddy roads.

While all of this was going on, the monks and peasants were standing by, watching, shaking their heads, saying or at least thinking: "There goes the neighborhood."

The only areas around Monte Cassino that were left relatively unfortified were the mountains to the east of the valley, those six thousand foot high Apennines, and a three hundred thirty-three yard (three hundred meter) circle around the Monastery itself. The Germans had respected the sanctity and the propaganda value of the historic building, and they would tell the world time and again that they were keeping the Abbey neutral, since they were the protectors of Western Culture, fighting a war against the God-less infidels with names like Churchy and F-Delano.

The Germans actually stuck to that promise, although that three-thirty-three yard radius tended to shrink as the battle grew longer and hotter. The Germans also weren't above storing bombs and munitions in caves much closer to the center of the Monastery than their press releases stated. Again and again they assured the monks that those munitions would be removed, but they were not.

And so, across the high rim above the *Liri* Valley, that Massif of Massacre, the Germans had constructed—anchored by the beautiful Monastery of Monte Cassino—a meat grinder.

***

Placed in charge of this elongated death trap was Panzer General Fridolin "Frido" vonSenger, Commander of the 14th Panzer Korps, with its seventy-five thousand battle-hardened men. Frido was a Rhodes Scholar, a gentleman who loved horses and Italians and hated to see either slaughtered by the battle that was to come. He realized there was a powerful difference between a soldier who had sworn to die for his country and a dumb animal or simple peasant who had not planned on dying at all. He had refused to carry out Nazi orders to kill Italian noncombatants. He hated to see any human being getting killed within his control, and he felt a twinge of heartache with every mule that died.

Frido had been one of those level heads who had tried to convince the bosses to fall back north of Rome, to fight the good fight from up in northern Italy. This seemed like a logical thing to do, but as we know, logic is an early casualty of war, right after truth.

Frido was a German to his very marrow, but he was no Nazi. He was bright enough to realize that Hitler's war was lost, but he was above all else a soldier. Some of his staff was later implicated in the plot to assassinate the Fuehrer. Their plan was never mentioned beforehand around the dinner table at Herr General's headquarters, but it was the elephant in the room—

looming even larger than the elephants that Hannibal had used to get to Rome by the sensible route centuries before.

You can picture the Fuehrer grasping vonSenger's face in both of his tightened hands, giving him a hard and oily kiss, mustache-brushing, and then telling him, "I know it was you, Frido. You broke my heart."

***

If Frido vonSenger had been more of a Hollywood Nazi, he would have been heard to say: "Let the Anglo-Yanks send forth as much young flesh as they can. Their tanks will be useless against us—sunken and mud-mired. As will be their trucks and armored vehicles. They will advance upon us in their naked innocence, bare, unprotected, their young bodies to be nothing more than meat and grizzle and bone upon the soil. Sustenance for our meat grinder."

But he wasn't, and didn't. He just kept his mouth shut and he waited.

***

Yes, for the Germans now it was simply a question of sitting behind their sited-in rifles and loaded and readied Spandau guns to await the arrival of the Allied invaders.

Their wait would not be a long one.

***

Chapter Four:
Texas Gun-slingers at the Red River

"Beautiful valley! Through those verdant meads
Unheard the Garigliano glides along;—
The Liris, nurse of rushes and of reeds,
The river taciturn of classic song."

-from "Monte Cassino" by Henry Wadsworth Longfellow 1875

***

Standing tall and erect in a farmhouse recently reconditioned into a warm and secure headquarters for his Fifth Army, the General who will be referred to as "Petoola" leaned over a map of the valley formed by the Rivers *Liri, Garigliano* and *Rapido*; he once again had called together his aides, cohorts and lackeys, and they were once again reviewing the plans to bust through Monte Cassino and then hop-skip all the way up into Rome. Rome had been Petoola's wet dream since before he ever set his foot in the Boot, and now the dream was about to be realized.

Petoola's Plan: As his Limey sidekicks created a diversion downstream by launching decoy attacks across the rivers of the *Liri* Valley, his 36th Division Texans (those proud, tough Texas boys with that sky-blue patch on their sleeve with the big Letter T, "*Yippi-tiii-yiii-yaaa!*") would, under cover of darkness, move down to the *Rapido* River (part of the *Rapido-Liri-Gariliano* river system), then hop across that river in small rafts and boats, to then quickly set up a series of Bailey Bridges for the tanks to roll across. After that, it remained simply to by-pass, outflank, or roll over the stationary German defense at Monte Cassino. Speed beats power, movement trumps immobility.

Petoola's officers gazed down at the table top, at the arrows drawn bold and thick on the war maps—neatly sketched on thick white paper by good old American fountain pen and by artists' brushes. The lines were inexorable in their ink—as neat and pure as a U.S. highway back home. *Roma*, here we come. The Eternal City would become the fountainhead for eternal glory for Petoola and—to a lesser extent of course—for his G.I.'s. Those who would survive, at least.

Only three things made this plan a half-assed invitation for butchery:

First, just getting across the *Liri* Valley to the river would be impossible. The troops would be slaughtered, decimated, by the well-positioned German artillery and defense gunners as they sat gazing down, waiting eagerly for their guests' arrival.

Second, making it across the deep, dark, muddy waters of the *Rapido* River itself would also be equally impossible; an exercise in blood-soaked nighttime confusion. The river banks were slick and long and slippery; the water was cold and dark and deep and hard-flowing. The other shore would be invisible, distant, unattainable, and perfectly defended.

Third, if a few lucky soldiers (*Lucky?*) actually did manage to make it across the river with their legs still attached to their bodies, with their bayonets and M-1's still at hand and operable, they would have nowhere to go, nothing to achieve, no idea what to do, no support from the rear, and no way of getting back across.

We review: Petoola's plan was perfect, except his men couldn't get to the river, couldn't get across it, and couldn't do anything even if they did.

And so Petoola rolled up the war maps and turned to his aides. "Sounds like a good one, amigos, let's call up the Brits, tell them it's a go, and tell them they'd better the hell hold up *their* end of this deal."

***

At the very least, this first battle of Monte Cassino, this Battle of the *Rapido* River, would force the Germans to pull troops away from the coast line, where they were suspecting a second Allied landing near the town of Anzio.

And at the very best, it would be front page, *New York Times*: Petoola standing at ram-rod attention in the back on an open troop transport, looking darn good, driving into Rome, left profile to the camera, grinning in black and white, but not grinning so much as to look un-heroic or un-General-ish.

***

Elsewhere, at least two high ranking Allies, Fred Walker and French General Juin, knew from the start that the plan was pure horseshit.

General Juin was a sawed-off little Frenchman who commanded a band of free-French, Moroccan and Algerian troops, now stationed to the east in the Apennines. Little Juin was "sawed-off" in more ways than one, having had his hand shot to shreds and then amputated during the last War. It cut down on the saluting. Juin was beloved by his men—a brave and crafty boss, anxious to redeem his countrymen from the debacle of their rolling over and playing dead before that Brown-Shirted stroll down the Champs Elysées in 1940.

He and his men had the grit and the brains to do just that—to avenge any past pockmark on their country's reputation. Although no one listened, the little French General—his cigar chomped tightly in his teeth and his beret flashing gold stars—had been lobbying for avoiding the valley attack altogether and instead bypassing the Germans by taking the mountain route around the right flank and then northward. Little Juin-bug's Moroccans and Algerians had been raised in mountains like these, had fought ferociously in North Africa, and—even though some of the tasks they would be given in Italy resembled climbing up the outside of the Eiffel Tower with full packs under heavy fire—they were up to the task. These guys were up for anything. They had something to prove, and they had the mules and the muscle to do it.

***

Fred Walker also knew early on that Petoola's plan was a hopeless and futile invitation to massacre. Fred was a General too, an American, but he had one less star on his hat than did Petoola, two to three, and Fred would be the guy responsible for sending these green and scared young Texans to their muddy and watery graves.

Fred had played this scene out once before, a quarter-century earlier, roles reversed, but with the details eerily similar. At the Marne, in the "War To End All Wars But Didn't Quite," Fred had been on the opposite shore, sitting pretty and mowing down advancing Germans like wheat with a thresher as the poor dumb bastards kept coming and coming, trying and trying to get across that dammed-up, damned and damning river.

But those slaughtered kids had been kids he didn't know, enemy kids, kids from a different world who had been bred to follow orders and die for the Fatherland. These kids dying today would be *his* kids, *his* Texans, or *his* ersatz Texans brought in when the real Texans had died, and it would be *their* mothers and sisters and wives that he would have to tell that their son/brother/husband offered up the ultimate sacrifice in a noble and worthwhile effort to protect his country. Except Fred knew that this effort was probably not noble and definitely not worthwhile.

But, two stars to three, what can you do, Fred wrote in his diary about how stupid the whole thing was, and then he got ready to send his men out to their certain death.

***

In wartime, once a career military man has reached the rank of General, from that point until peace talks he is basically playing with house money. His chips are the lives of his young soldiers. If he allows sentiment to enter into his game—allows himself to think of the empty houses and bank accounts and lives, or of the blood-soaked beds in camphor-smelling V.A. Hospitals—then the General starts prevaricating, and his game suffers, grows too cautious. Ultimately he is labeled as soft, weak, still in the game but without *game*. A butterfly, a pussy-whip. And his career plans stall out at Brigadier.

But if he can just put aside those emotions that make him human, if he can allow sleep to come to him without visions of hollow-eyed wives and mothers and brave but befuddled Dads and kids, then he may advance in his career, get that second star, then a third, maybe even a fourth…and maybe…maybe…(dare he even think it?)…a statue in some park somewhere! That ultimate glory of a leaden form covered daily with pigeon poop.

***

So the Allied General Petoola convinced himself that the plan would work. Men would die, but that's what men come to war to do, that's why they got onboard the Kaiser-built Liberty Ship back in New York harbor. To come over here and to die for their country.

This plan would positively *blast* Petoola's Fifth Army over Monte Cassino, squashing Germans like soggy mushrooms underneath a steamroller, and then: northward toward Rome. This plan would work. People would be rewarded. The three-pronged attack would shatter the Gustav Line like Joe Louis's fist hitting Max Schmeling's chin.

The brave men in service to the General would somehow manage to get across the bottom of the *Liri* Valley, then to ford the river system and keep advancing over the top of the Monte Cassino ridge, and onward, onward, Christian Soldiers. From then on, the only sight Americans would have of the rivers *Rapido* and *Liri* and *Garigliano* would be in review mirrors and old history books.

These British blokes were polite, sneaky, untrustworthy, but if they could simply attack the River in two waves down stream so the Germans were busy trying to drive them back south, if they could simply take the high ground on the U.S. flank, then the Americans could launch a main attack across the *Rapido* that would catch German Panzer General Frido vonSenger und Etterlin with his pants down around his ankles and his *Neblewerfer* rockets in the dirt beside his feet.

Petoola had visions of his men (his chips) sweeping across the Valley, across Monte Cassino, and all the way to another star on his shoulder and dinner in the White House for honored guests only. And at the very least, this attack would force the Germans to take troops away from Anzio, where the Allies were landing in an amphibious attack that would grab more headlines than all this messy foot-traffic in the south. "See?" he could tell the press, "See what my army made possible?"

The first British attack would take the Germans' mind off the *Liri* Valley, and the second would grab the high ground above the Valley and give some cover to the Americans with their third wave.

To Petoola and his band of tunnel-visioned visionaries, the whole thing looked awful good on paper.

This plan would work.

***

No.

Right off, things went as wrong as they could go. The Brits' two attacks—the one for diversion, and the one designed to take the high ground so they could cover the Yanks' river-crossing—both quickly deflated and flattened into failure.

After the Germans were quickly surprised, the plenty-aforementioned German Panzer General Frido vonSenger und Etterlin (his name plate alone weighed four pounds) talked his fellow officer, Field Marshall "Smiling Albert" Kesselring (for once, that is history's choice of a nickname, not mine) into lending some of his troops to drive the pesky Brits back across the Valley.

"Jeez, I don't know, Frido, we really need the guys over here, we're getting ready to repulse this coastal invasion and all."

"Well, okay, Smiling Al, I'm just saying, our intelligence is telling us not to worry about the amphib, that it's not coming. On the other hand, when somebody tells the Fuehrer that his beloved Gustav Line has been busted, and he asks how in the hell did *that* happen, and we have to tell him, well, Smiling Al wouldn't lend us any troops, so…"

"How many you need?"

The inaccurate intelligence about no Anzio landing being imminent was the work of the head of German military intelligence, a guy named Canaris—Admiral Wilhelm Canaris—but he was later executed for plotting to kill the Fuehrer, so—Who Ya Gonna Trust?

With Smiling Al's borrowed troops at his disposal, Frido was easily able to smash back the British invasion.

You already know that this guy Frido was smart; so like any good military man or chess player, he could think a few moves into the future. But he didn't like to do that too often because every time he looked too far into the future, he saw the same writing on the same wall— No way in Hades was Germany going to win this war. That dream had been starved out and burned to ash at Stalingrad. All Frido and his buddies were doing now was playing out the string, although a few of his thicker-thinking buddies hadn't managed to figure all that out yet.

Playing out the string by trying to kill more of the enemy than they were killing of yours. Hopeless, stupid, soul-destroying, but Frido took a breath and commenced killing the Limeys trying to slog their way across his river.

***

The night was draped in a heavy fog, the river current was twisting and sinking the Brits' boats, the well-positioned German artillery was raining down, so all the Brits could do was turn around, go back across, lick their wounds, collect their dead, and search for someone to provide a spot of tea.

So: the Brits could provide no diversion for the soon-to-come Texan assault. They had also not managed to gain any control of any high ground. As anyone with one good eye could now see, the Texans would be crawling and rowing and staggering into a Valley of Death, with the British back at camp, bleeding and breathing hard and looking around for some Tennyson to read.

***

The Brits had seen hundreds of their comrades and officers blown to pieces ever since their landing at Salerno. Now they were a sorry mixture of battle-weary and sweaty-faced kids. In December the Yanks had robbed them of their Christmas turkeys; now the Germans had robbed them of any hope for a Happy New Year.

Their first wave didn't even have the benefit of artillery cover, since the officers had decided to maintain the element of surprise.

First, the Brits had to slog their way across a soggy plain where the Germans had removed all trees and bushes that could obstruct their line of fire; landmines had been planted instead of shrubbery. The attackers were lugging little amphibious crafts to get across the currents of the river. Engineers had marked safe paths through the mine fields with white tape, but the tape had become invisible in the darkness and shredded at many points by the German artillery. Minefield guides had been promised but never appeared.

Mines were blowing off feet and legs while mortar and artillery fire was sailing down from above. The series of hills and cliffs had made the valley into an echo chamber so that each explosion would echo and re-echo, one terrible killing sound overlapping the next. It gave the impression of never-ending artillery, which was pretty much true.

A few Brits got confused, got half away across the water, only to get twisted around, landed on the same bank from which they had left, and started firing on their countrymen, thinking they were Nazi defenders in the dark.

Many of the tightly packed amphibious crafts were overturned in the river by mortar fire and the current. Men with lead-heavy packs were tossed into the murky, cold water.

There's this: Washed-out Englishmen trying to swim back to shore felt the hands of their fellow soldiers grabbing and clutching at their legs in an effort to get above water. Only thing to do: kick yourself free and keep swimming. That would be a sensation to haunt one for a lifetime. The nightmare's soundtrack would be the screams of those soldiers fortunate enough to be dying *above* the waterline.

British ferries, rafts and boats were still attempting to get men and supplies across the river. Attempts were still being made to set up Bailey Bridges—those Erector Set like devices that could support tanks and heavy equipment. But German artillery put an end to that plan.

The Germans forced some unarmed Italian peasants, at gunpoint, to go out to meet the invaders so that their exact position could be determined in order to hone in the mortar fire and Eighty-eights and artillery. The British did what war forced you to do— they shot and killed the peasants as they approached.

***

The Brits' Essex battalion was a collection of East Enders out of London—called themselves Swede-bashers, Fishmongers— who had been hardened by the nighttime rainy season of V-1s and V-2 in the late 1930s, but nothing could prepare a man for a night like they had just lived through…or died during.

Having cool names like "the Black Cat Division" and 'The Royal Fusiliers" didn't seem to matter if you were unable to hold your position, unable to advance, and unable to retreat because your "Allies" were bombing you by mistake with all the modern artillery shells that American munitions factories could mass produce. And your dying buddy was grabbing at your legs from beneath the water.

A letter home to London: "I have changed a good deal. I cannot smile now."

Nor perhaps ever again.

Yet raw resiliency is packed into that British bone marrow along with that British reserve. A young Corps Gunner named Spike Milligan was wounded and blasted into shellshock, and then disciplined for not staying healthy. Uncontrollable sobbing and stuttering had replaced his usual jokes and easy speech. Back in the medical tent, he told a doctor that he couldn't figure out why he couldn't stop crying. The doctor called him a coward, tranquilized him, and shipped him out alone.

Somehow, after years, Spike was able to recover his mind and his sense of humor, and after the war joined Peter Sellers and others to form a surrealistically funny group called the Goon Show, which was a precursor to Beyond the Fringe and eventually—Monty Python. A direct Limey line running from bomb-loony at Monte Casino to the Dead Parrot skit. Yes, they have some resilient sense of humor, those Brits do.

***

But resiliency does not mean success; so the English plan to divert German attention from the Yanks' attempted river crossing and to provide high ground cover for the Yanks had been a complete failure.

The Germans held control of all the ground around the valley. The conventional wisdom of warfare said an army had to have a six-to-one advantage to displace a heavily entrenched enemy. The valley was flooded, marshy and free of protection. It would be senseless suicide for the Americans to attempt a river crossing now.

***

"Still a go, sir?"

"Still a go."

"Even with the Brits gone nowhere?"

"We don't need them. Pussies."

Petoola ordered the crossing.

General Fred wrote that he knew of no attempted river cross under direct enemy fire that had succeeded. Ever. In history.

Fred sent Petoola a message trying to explain this.

Petoola sent back his Best Wishes for a Fine Campaign.

Under his breath General Fred cursed Petoola and sent his boys off to their certain death.

***

The grunts of the Texas 36th could see the same thing that Fred saw. They sat and gazed across that dark valley—denuded now, swampy, flooded by the Germans. No place to run to, no place to hide. And they spoke of things other than what was coming, of what the night would bring.

***

Mack: I never thought I'd feel bad about leaving that little slit trench of ours, but when they told us to move out, I wanted to stay right where I was, with my iron rations and atabrine tablets and my saltpeter.

Scooter: They gave us the saltpeter to keep our minds on the battle.

Mack: Hard to miss.

Scooter: We were such kids, could barely call us young men.

Mack: I wouldn't have minded if they planted acorns and we waited for them to grow into trees before we moved out.

***

On the night of January 20, 1944, at twenty hundred hours, the American grunts set out to do battle. They were loaded up with their own equipment, as well as rubber rafts and a fleet of four hundred pound wooden boats, along with the materials to build tank bridges across the river. They had to carry all of this back-busting weigh more than a thousand yards under heavy enemy fire.

***

Scooter: Dumb, dumb, dumb. The rubber rafts had been all ripped to hell by artillery anyway, most of them useless. And, what did it take, four of us, one on each corner, to haul those wooden monstrosities, didn't it?

Mack: In the pitch dark, except for a Very Light now and then, and the unfriendly light of unfriendly artillery.

Scooter: Us there staggering around, slushing, stumbling around in the dark, falling, getting up, like some circus clowns, getting lost, hauling that damn wooden rowboat. I dug splinters for years.
Mack: We looked like…we were about as efficient as that Stan and Ollie movie, where they're hauling a piano across a little rope footbridge, in the Alps, a thousand feet up…
Scooter: And they meet a gorilla, coming the other way.
Mack: We met some gorillas too.

***

Gorillas of hot, flesh-piercing lead. In the darkness and the fog, battalions got lost and disoriented, like the British had—Which way is that god-damn river?—and as they twisted in circles of confusion, trying to relocate—all that noise gave the Germans a target area for the mortars, artillery, machineguns, and the Screaming Meemies.

Try lugging a four hundred pound wooden boat along with your fifty pound pack through a swampy minefield with artillery shells popping all around you. It's a wonder any soldier advanced at all, but they did. Both the combat-hardened vets and the kids who had just finished Basic—Texans and wanna-be Texans alike—they all somehow kept slogging forward that night.

***

Mack: Schmeisser fire, Screaming Meemies, and I never wanted to be a fucken Texan to begin with. I was just some scared-shitless kid from Brooklyn.
Scooter: We were young. Then…

***

When a few American troops actually managed to reach the river's edge and tried to launch, the boats would slide down the slippery shore, only to twist sideways and immediately take on water and then sink. Others went under because artillery had punctured the sides. Still others were ripped apart and out of the nervous and numbed hands of the soldiers. Some boats made the voyage halfway across the river before being blown out of the water by the shelling. The exhausted men with their fifty pound packs were tossed into the water. The river was twelve feet deep in places. Plenty room down there for dead, drowned colleague, and plenty room for you to join them. *Come on it, the water's fine.*

Some battalions wisely got lost for the night—never even got close to the *Rapido* River, which was now turning a blood-soaked red; instead they decided to dig some foxholes in the muck and stay alive. The engineers had attempted to create some clean paths by building "corduroy roads" of log lengths, but they made the foot soldiers trek no easier.

A few poor souls actually made it to the other side of the river, where they were sitting ducks for the German shooting gallery. The Germans were dug in within their trenches and bunkers, five machinegun nests had been equally strung out across the bluff. Four self-propelled guns bore down on the helpless Texans—compliments of General Hans Bessel and his meticulous Arian planning. The Germans fired at will. Will and his colleagues shit in their pants.

***

Scooter: And you'd try to be discrete about it, get it all cleaned up before your buddies saw. Every time.

***

As a radioman ducked low, cranked up his field phone, and managed to establish radio contact with Command, he asked for…then pleaded for…a retreat order for the four hundred stranded victims on the German side of the river. When no retreat order was received, they came back anyway.

If a battalion had started out with one hundred fifty men and four officers, they were lucky to get back with an officer or two and maybe fifteen men.

The men were exhausted, decimated, shell shocked, confused, demoralized, and totally disheartened.

So…as the sun appeared the next morning, Petoola gave them the order to attack again.

This time would be different. This time would be in sunlight, so that the Germans would have no trouble at all sighting them in. So this time would be worse than last night. Nervous junior officers told their men that failure was not an option, that this time the Gustav Line would be smashed. No one believed a word of it; not the pale and nervous officers, not their twitching men.

Some C.O.'s began crying as they watched their men head out that morning. Didn't know too many of their names any more, didn't matter…just knew that they wouldn't be coming back.

And for this daylight attack there would be one added roadblock—the bodies of your fellow soldiers, piled six and seven deep along your path. There was not a remote chance of building a footbridge or a Bailey Bridge. There were no boats to get across the river, no communication, no smoke cover, no indications of where the landmines were placed, no way to dig a foxhole in the mud, no sanity, no sense, no end to the bewilderment and the insanity.

The mission failed.

***

The total of American lives destroyed in this early little engagement at Monte Cassino was one thousand, six hundred eighty-one. Total gain by Allied troops—none.

Both sides declared a truce, long enough to collect their dead. Each army helped the other, lent stretchers, did the heavy lifting, not paying attention to uniforms or stripes. They weren't really collecting bodies so much—not whole ones—just pieces mostly. Feet, arms, cocks, a lot of unrecognizable chunks of meat and bone. Dog tags. Sometime a human face, frozen forever in fear.

The two enemy sides worked together, helped each other out, fuck Petoola, fuck the Fuehrer: "Oh yeah, so you got a relative in Brooklyn? What's the name? What part of Brooklyn? I got an aunt and uncle close to there. Prospect Park, well, can you beat that. I'll tell them when I write. Here, here, a smoke, take it." Kill ya later.

***

Petoola blamed the British for the failure of his master plan. If they had fought like men in their earlier assignment of getting across the river, the American plan would have been a success. It was those weak-kneed Limeys who had caused all of this fiasco.

After the war, some of Petoola's men demanded a Congressional investigation into this bloody incompetence. An officer testified, "I had one hundred eighty-four men…forty-eight hours later I had seventeen. If that's not mass murder, I don't know what is." Petoola had more friends on the Hill than did the veterans; he was exonerated. Most of the tired vets had figured that he would be. That is the way things work.

***

Petoola pointed out that during the attack, a few of the troops had miraculously somehow made their way up the Massif, all the way to Monte Calvary—the stone of Snake's Head Ridge—Military name Hill or Point 593—managing to climb to a point less than two thousand yards from the Monastery itself, before being beaten back by German reinforcements.

In the end, anyone who came back at all was right back where he had started. Repeat those numbers: In the *Rapido* River attack alone, the one thousand, six hundred and eighty-one American men had died for no gain whatsoever. How many friends do you have? How many people can you name? Fifty? A hundred? One thousand, six hundred and eighty-one?

The men had been whipped and worked like rented mules, and sixteen hundred of them had died a mule's death. Nothing had been accomplished.

Some patriots started thinking differently about things.

Who were the men in all of this, they wondered, and who were the mules?

***

Chapter Five:
"We're all of us Mules."

"…was that day's disgrace
The Pontiff's only, or in part thine own?"

-from "Monte Cassino" by Henry Wadsworth Longfellow 1875

***

Mack: Let's face it, we were all of us mules. Mules down there.
Scooter: Pretty much. If it wasn't for the real mules, the *mule-mules*, then that battle couldn't've been fought. No.
Mack: No.
Scooter: So much mud, so much rock.
Mack: I still find dirt between my toes sometimes.
Scooter: That's new mud, Mack, that's from your grapes, that's not Monte Cassino mud, buddy.
Mack: Maybe not, it still brings me back there. Those poor, god-damn mules. I mean the real ones. Remember how they used to

get so scared? Poor, dumb things. They couldn't figure out what was going on.

Scooter: Us either, but sure, what did those know about artillery. You couldn't just say to them, "No, baby, at ease, those are *our* guns. Those are *ours*."

Mack: Wouldn't matter anyway. Our guns killed as many of us as theirs did anyway.

Scooter: You ever tell anyone about that night?

Mack: What night?

Scooter: You know.

Mack: What night?

Scooter: You know.

Combined laughter.

Mack: Yeah, I'm sure my daughter—fourteen year old kid—would understand. "Listen, honey, your Daddy and this other guy, we packed ourselves together in a sangar for the night, his god-damn crotch stuck in my face like a catcher's mitt, my god-damn crotch stuck in his. Just two guys just trying to say warm. Just trying to get away from the guns. Things were different in such a situation. Sixty shells a minute busting outside, echoes overlapping echoes. No decent water or food. Jesus."

Scooter: No sex.

Mack: Definitely no hanky-panky. Didn't need the saltpeter even. Just two guys trying to stay warm. Stay alive. Yeah, she'd understand all that all right.

Scooter: The things you wind up doing, huh? I remember more than one time, carrying a pack, some mule would panic from the sounds, just leap right off the side. Screaming all the way down. The screaming almost human, like it finally understood everything. The sound of it just fading away, down, down. Never knew a mule could scream like that. You have to feel sorry for them, huh? What the hell did they know? I mean, we didn't know much, they didn't tell us much, just, "Go get your heinie shot off, it's for your country," but mules, they didn't even tell them that much.

Mack: They only talked Italian anyway.

Scooter: No one ever explained to them why they were being tortured, killed, blown apart. I mean, a lot of guys—our guys—you know what they did, got to be too much for them to handle, you shoot yourself in the foot, that's all, you're done, you're out. Shoot off a toe, side of your upper leg, whatever.

Mack: Nothing important.

Scooter: No, right, always something you could do without. But the poor mules, they couldn't even do that for themselves. No self-mutilating mules.

Mack: We were all of us mules.

***

Mules were precisely what both armies in southern Italy needed that winter; the animals were tough, dumb, strong, and surefooted. Followed orders; they did what they were asked, no questions. With perfect body types for carrying loads up, down, and around the rocky hills and mountain paths. Bringing up supplies, food, water, medicines, batteries, ammo, equipment. To come back down with dead bodies and parts of the same—that's about the only things worth retrieving after a firefight. They were long-legged, could slog through mud that would immobilize a truck or a tank. Steady of foot and purpose, usually, on the ten-inch wide rock paths that were notched into the mountain sides. They could focus on one stubborn thing—just getting there and back—even with explosions all about.

Both sides scoured the country for healthy mules, took them from the farmer-peasants. "I need! I need for my farm, my farm. I gotta keep, for the farm, for me, please. To plow. I use to plow, I need. Please. *Per favore*."

"This is wartime, *gum-bah*. Get used to it."

One mule could pack and carry two hundred pounds of ammunition, water, K-rations—booze too, a lot of it, wine and rum, used for sedatives, disinfectant, mostly just to get screaming, wide-eyed drunk on. Then packing those useless pieces of flesh, coming back down, heading for a pillow case and a prayer in a foreign cemetery.

"I need for the farm. I no have mule, the farm, she die. *I die*."

"C'mon, pop, you come too. We can use some good muleskinners. Slave labor is not out of the question at all."

Peasants were kidnapped—you can call it "appropriated," you call can call it "commandeered"—but peasants were kidnapped, by both sides, used as skinners until the war killed them off, along with their animals. Annihilated by an artillery hit, blown off the side of a mountain. Left there to die slow.

***

Mack: At least they died close to home. We were dying too, but halfway around the world. Scoot, you ever eat a dead mule?

Scooter: Naw, not that I know of. You?

Mack: Plenty guys did though.

Scooter: I know they did. We were hungry.

Mack: All the time. Hungry, wet, dirty, and scared. Once in awhile horny.

Scooter: (Singing) I got my mule to keep me warm.

Mack: You know, all those rotting mule carcasses, all those rotting G.I. carcasses, all those rotting Nazis, I bet to this day that fucken valley is the most fertile land on Earth. Best farming dirt in Italy, don't you think?

Scooter: Could be. Except for the malaria and dysentery we left them with.

Mack: Blood too. All that blood, animal and human, good for the soil, I'd think. Twenty thousand dead guys bleeding themselves dry into the good earth. Plus, one hell of a lot of mule juice, mule blood. Blood can act as your best fertilizer. Full of nutrients.

Scooter: Sure. But all their urine and their spit, not so much.

Mack: Okay, but how about their shit then? That'd be good. How much you want to bet those fucken peasants to this day they're thanking us for coming over there. For making their land so fertile. The few of them that survived, at least, how much you want to bet they mention us in their prayers every night, whenever the crops come in.

Scooter: Glad to know America helped them out.

Mack: "Dear Mrs. Jones: The War Department regrets to inform you that your son was all blown to hell in some shitty little town in southern Italy, but you should feel proud and honored that his body rotted itself into some of the finest farmland in the entire Mediterranean area. Your boy is grapes and olives now. Be proud."

***

The mules' feet suffered from the elements, and also from lack of basic equipment—shoes and nails.

***

Mack: What about *our* feet? The Trench Foot? I saw guys with feet so big they couldn't get them in their boots anymore. Had to wrap them up in rags, go on walking.

***

And the mules often cut the strung telephone lines with their ragged hoofs.

***

Mack: The mules didn't care about the damn phone lines. But whenever they stepped on a landmine, well, that was a different story. They paid attention then.

***

The Gurkhas—those incredibly tough soldiers out of Nepal—were as unbelievably cavalier about their mules' lives as they were about their own. More about their human sacrifice later, but on one single night only twenty of two hundred mules might survive a journey hauling supplies up to the soldiers. In a Tunisian trip, in a mule train of eighty, two made it back. Two. The rest killed by mortar and machinegun fire. This was common. Very common statistics—there are a hundred other stats just like it—but it doesn't matter.

***

Mack: A lot of dead mule meat.

***

Many were castrated by landmine.

***

Mack: Well, that didn't matter, don't you know—mules can't reproduce? They're half-horse, half-donkey, all-dumb, all-tough, not quite as stubborn as their rep says. And as sterile as a mortar shell. You want another mule, you got to go get yourself another horse, introduce him to another donkey.

Scooter: (Crooning) "Another sunny, honey-moon…"

***

It was often a fourteen hour round trip to bring supplies up to the front, wherever the front happened to be that day, and then to get back. Fourteen hours of being targeted by German hot metal. The mules were too oblivious to ever turn around and go home, but sometimes their handlers did, if they figured they could get away with it and not get court marshaled or—if they were civilian—executed. On the spot.

One night a British soldier who was using mules to carry supplies for the battle front came face-to-face with the Monastery, up-close. The path had started out much too rocky for even a Jeep, and then shrank into a mountainside path barely eighteen inches across. The soldier was leading a convoy of three mules—he could have used thirty—with an Arab handler running them. To the right side of the foot-and-a-half wide path was a sheer drop down the mountainside, a drop to death. To their left was the rock wall. Between a rock and a hard place, not knowing which was which.

When they started getting bombarded by fire—it was friendly fire, but who cares—one mule, top heavy with the weight of spare radio batteries, twitched away from the noise, lost its footing, slipped and fell off the ledge. Never had a chance. The mules and the men—all of them wet, sleep-deprived, blinded by the night and by the artillery flashes, pressed on and finally delivered their cargo. Nobody was impressed. This happened so often it barely qualifies as a story.

***

Mack: The mules never got shellshock, battle fatigue, bomb-loony, bomb-drunk, brain dead, or "Don't give a shit any more" happy. Hell, they started out that way. With us soldier boys, it took a couple months for all that to start to happen.
Scooter: Evolution. The mules were more evolved than we were.

***

Animals become supremely disposable in any combat area. The Germans would take sheep and lamb from the monks living in the monetary. They'd offer to pay the monks a few *lire*, then fork over even less, and have themselves some mutton for supper. The monks weren't able to care for or to feed the animals anyway, so they didn't offer resistance. Cows too.

Sheep and goats would be driven through minefields to test the area. After a hit, they were lunch.

***

Mack: We were all turned into animals.
Scooter: The New Zealanders—what do they call them now, Kiwis?...

***

That is the current colloquialism.

***

Mack: Back then, a "Kiwi" was an Airman who didn't fly, like the bird, remember that term, Scooter?
Scooter: Right. But what I wanted to say about these New Zealanders, they fought like they were animals too. Like the Gurkhas did. Very tough guys. You'd hear about a bunch of Kiwis crawling forward under MG fire, they'd crawl up to a string of barbed wire, the first couple grunts would flop their bodies on the wire, lie flat so their mates could use them as footbridges, get over the wire. My God. That's animal behavior right there.

Mack: Everybody was a mule. Yeah, then somebody'd finally use wire cutters, but that didn't help the bellies of those first few bleeding suckers, did it?

Scooter: Not much.

Mack: That's what I mean by us all being…we were all too dumb to save ourselves. It's like those army of ants you hear about. They come up to a stream to cross, the first eight million of them run into the water so that they'll drowned and float and so their bodies will be the floating pontoon bridges for the rest of the army behind them. It's crazy. It's nonhuman nature.

Scooter: It's nuts, all of it is.

Mack: But we do it. We do it.

Scooter: Well, we *did* it. Our nonhuman nature coming out. They say a real hero is either a drunk or an idiot.

Mack: We saw a lot of idiots, but we saw a lot of drunks too, didn't we? Lot a good old, homemade wine in those farmhouses we passed by, coming up from Sicily.

Scooter: Rum too sometimes. Hard stuff once in awhile, if you could find it. Not much of it escaped us.

Mack: Nope. Not too much. And you know the Krauts had their share of *schnapps* in those bunkers of theirs. Some of those bunkers they made were so secure they wouldn't even interrupt their Cribbage games when our artillery started zeroing in. They didn't care. "Pass the *schnapps*, Hans, deal the cards."

Scooter: And the Poles.

Mack: The Polacks? You think they would have had that final attack up to the Monastery—what was left of it, what was left of *them*—if they hadn't been drunk as a skunk on New Years? What you said is the truth—the real hero is either an idiot or a drunk.
Scooter: Or a mule.
Mack: All of us.

***

The French General Alphonse Juin—you remember him—he was one who appreciated the value of the mules.

Much of the horror of 1944 could have been avoided, including the destruction of the sacred Monastery, if the Allied commanders had taken the advice of that wise little Pepsi. Sure, the French fighting man got that bad rap as pansies when their country fell so quickly in 1940, but from that nadir on, Juin's French proved to be as tough, smart, and brave as anyone, even the Germans.

And that was Juin all over—especially the part about being smart, smart about his men and his mules. He had almost no tanks or heavy vehicles at his disposal, but the guy had mules, plenty of them. Picked them up whenever, wherever he could grab them. He went to school on Hannibal and his elephants and little Juen figured this: Why not bypass the cesspool of death and the Abbey altogether? Why not head north through the Abruzzi Mountains instead? Using mules. Yes, the track would be desolate, steep, rocky, dangerous, but it was by far the least fortified stretch of the Gustav Line. Better to be moving forward with surefooted mules and your troops not being fired upon, better than being stuck in the mud with a million dollar tank while the enemy picked you off one by one from up on the high ground.

The truth was: One mule was worth at least twelve tanks in southern Italy. One dumb animal worth more than a dozen fancy Pentagon machines. But you couldn't tell that to those West Point boys. You get a bunch of Allied commanders in a room, you say to them, "Tanks," then say to them, "Mules," and you know what their answer will be, even before you ask a question. "Ol' Blood'n'Guts" George Patton leading a brigade of mules? Petoola mucking up his John Wayne image with critters that are stupid and funny looking and go "He-haw, he-haw," and can't even screw? Won't ever happen.

***

Mack: I said they can't *reproduce*. I'm not sure if they can screw or not.
Scooter: They do okay, huh. Under the right circumstances.
Mack: And they didn't say, "He-haw" all that much, the ones I was familiar with. You had to be quiet on those soirees. Let the Germans know where you were and you got your ass bombed off. I figured it was almost like those mules knew they had to stay silent or else.
Scooter: Maybe they weren't so dumb then, either.
Mack: No dumber than us. Both them and us hung around for the duration. That was dumb.
Scooter: Where else you gonna go?

Mack: Sweden maybe? Mars?

Scooter: Mule R and R sites? I don't know. Shoot your foot off.

Mack: Well, I thought about it, we all did at some point. Trouble was, then you'd have to spend an awful lot of years lying. Lying to yourself, to an awful lot of people who couldn't understand.

***

On the way up to the front, the mules were often walking time bombs because they would be transporting hand grenades or other explosives. This meant that they would only have to suffer an indirect hit from mortar or artillery fire in order to ignite their load. Phosphorus burns. This didn't do much for the confidence of the accompanying soldiers or the Italian handlers either.

On the way back down, the body bags and body parts were never very fresh, more gruesome than the supplies they were bringing up, but less explosive, at least.

***

Scooter: Those Englishmen had such a way of stating stuff, didn't they? They wouldn't say that the poor mules were being smashed to crap all the time, no, they'd report that there was an "ever dwindling number of animals."

Mack: "An ever dwindling number," huh? Same as us. There was an "ever dwindling number" of us too.

Scooter: That there was.

***

There are times you just can't win. When our Flying Fortresses and Liberator bombers were destroying the town of

Monte Cassino—the *town* I'm talking about now, not the Monastery itself (more about that later)—some of these "pinpoint bombing exercises" landed directly on the British 27th Battalion. Killed "friendly" officers, gunners, men wounded and dead, wiped out a Moroccan casualty clearing station, some Italian mule handlers and, here's the point, wounded a bunch of mules. Just wounded them, not killed.

That meant that some poor Brit had to walk among the ruins, find the hopelessly wounded animals, and he had to shoot fifteen of them, one after the other—bam, bam, bam.

These were almost pets to him by now—friends—but they're all lying there, all chewed up by the explosions, can't stand up, making sad and quiet sounds, whimpering, looking up at him for help—mules have big eyes—but he never looked away. Said he looked each one of them in the eye as he fired.

So if the Germans weren't exterminating these poor animals, the guys on their side were dropping bombs on them, and if they survived that—wounded—then their master would come along and put them out of their military with a bullet to the brain.

See what I mean? You just can't win.

***

Scooter: Remember Spence? A guy named Spencer?
Mack: No. Who?
Scooter: He comes back from a mule run one morning. He's covered with—with what we don't know. Looking bloody, red, but with big chunks of hair all over the guy too. Big, dirty chunks

and clumps of thick hair. "Spence, what happened to you. You're wounded." "No," he says to us, "No, I'm not. A Meemie or a mine got the mule I was with. Damn thing exploded all over me. I'm fine." And he was too. He made it all the way, I think. I don't know where he is now. I should look him up. But that morning, coming back in, you'd swear he was the Abominable Snowman. Big Foot. And smelling? Terrible. The blood, mule blood, flesh, mule flesh.

Mack: The shit too, I would imagine.

Scooter: I'm sure, yeah. I don't remember that. We washed him off though. We hosed him off, after, he was fine. "Let me back at 'em."

***

Spencer was lucky that the mule meat he was covered in was fresh. So many carcasses, men and mule, littered the mountain sides that the buzzing of flies and the scurrying of rats would keep men awake at night. Dysentery spread from man to man, platoon to platoon. A soldier would step on a dead mule during the day, get the disease on his boot, be coughing and dying and spreading by sundown.

***

Mack: We were all of us mules. Us and them and the I-tals too, dying of pneumonia, never walking again cause our feet got swelled up three times the size by Trench Foot, we'd get gangrene, they'd send us up a little peroxide, tell us, "Put this on, it'll help." You wouldn't treat an animal that way. Well, you would. They did. All mules, human and not, enemy, foe, friend, all of us. A third of us were killed by our own artillery, misdirected. Who cared? That's what we all were to them. Only difference was, some of us were alive, most of us wound up dead. But every single one of us was mules.

Scooter: Yeah, to some of the brass, that's what we were too, I suppose. True. Churchill would tell the press we were just standing around, watching the Russians doing all the fighting. But in his defense, Petoola…

Mack: Oh, fucken Petoola, please don't get me started on that guy.

***

Next, we'll talk about that guy.

***

Chapter Six:
The General Known as Petoola

"...a child of fancy and of fiction at the best!"

-from "Monte Cassino" by Henry Wadsworth Longfellow 1875

***

Scooter: You have to remember, the guy had a hopeless, impossible job cut out for him down there. Nobody could've handled it without any mistakes. Nobody could've done it at all.
Mack: Brought it on himself.

***

A combination of prenatal factors made the General we know as "Petoola" into what he was—what he was to become. He sprang from one of those khaki-blankets-on-all-the-beds military/divinity families, a forefather had been a General in the American Revolutionary War, his father a career military man, his cousin was no less a patriot than General George Marshall himself. After high school, Petoola naturally and expectantly went off to

West Point, having received his appointment at the age of seventeen, which might say something about outside influence or internal drive. He graduated one hundred tenth out of a hundred thirty-nine, so there were few early indications he would become one of the three or four most important officers in the most important war that our most important country ever got itself importantly involved in.

The First World War began smoking, conveniently, soon after all those Second Lieutenant hats got sent sailing up into the air above the Point at Commencement, and Petoola got himself wounded in the Vosges Mountains—not much known about that, but at a young age the guy had already seen and felt and smelled combat.

Between wars his career seemed to have stalled out. He was immobilized at the rank of Captain for an interminable sixteen years—that's a lot of promotion cycles missed, nearly as long as some entire military careers—a period during which he had different nondescript jobs and appointments—including Deputy Commissioner of the Civilian Conservation Corps out in Omaha, Nebraska.

***

Mack: That was about his level, that's where he should've stayed. Keep him clearing brush and making nature trails for the kids, instead of calling the shots at Operation Torch. Operation Torch, my ass…he sure torched *my* ass…what a screw-up.
Scooter: Anybody would've. That Fifth Army of his…

Mack: "Petoola's" Fifth Army, please. You know he always insisted in the papers it would have his name in the title. No, no, never just "the Fifth Army," had to be "*Petoola's* Fifth Army."

Scooter: Was *our* Fifth Army as much as his, but oh yeah, the man liked his ink, I'm not denying that.

Mack: Publicity hound. Got drunk with it. Needed the flame of fame, fame, fame, all the time. Guy made Patton look like a recluse, a shrinking hermit. Yup, made "Blood'n'Guts" look as shy and retiring as old Saint Benedict himself.

Scooter: True, true, but what I started to say here is, the Fifth Army…

Mack: "*Petoola's* Fifth Army."

Scooter: O*ur* Fifth Army, the *Fighting Man's* fifth army. It was us doing the heavy lifting, huh? …the heavy bleeding, I know, but anyway, it wasn't really a single army at all. It was a bunch of armies, in reality. It was a polyglot army.

Mack: A what?

Scooter: Different languages. Heterogeneous. You're the words man, big time newspaper guy. You ever look at a dictionary?

Mack: Oh, heterogeneous. You should've said that to begin with.

Scooter: Fewer than half of us were Americans. Was a dozen different countries tossed together. How can anyone run an army like that? And Petoola had to deal with all of it. Men and officers, Brits, Yanks, Frenchies, Poles, Indians, the Gurkhas…

Mack: Just Brits, Kiwis and Irishmen alone—that's four-five different language right there. Then you add in your Japs—I mean *American* Japs—loyal Japs, Japanese I mean...

Scooter: That'd be an impossible situation for any General to deal with, huh?

Mack: Guy could be an asshole in five different languages at once.

***

The American Nisei 110th Infantry was made up of Americans of Japanese decent.

***

Mack: Those who hadn't been hauled off to Prisoner of War camps outside Hollywood. Third generation Americans...

Scooter: There were even some Brazilians in the Fifth, and the North Africans, Tunisia...

Mack: So now that's *fifty-five* different languages right there. I wonder what Tunisians speak?

Scooter: Yanks alone had a bunch of different languages. Remember when we first met, us two back in Basic?

Mack: Sure. I didn't know what the hell you were talking about half the time. You with your "pop," "Let's go have a bottle of 'pop.'" What the hell?

Scooter: The first time you talked about getting a pie, I'm thinking, "The guy wants an apple pie? What for?"

Mack: Pizza.

Scooter: Yeah, well, pizza, now I know, I understand. But there's poor Petoola in charge of all these different armies, nobody knows anybody, never even heard of half the countries each other had come from, the various Generals all not trusting each other— "Those Limies, can't trust them, and take a look at those dark-skinned Indians over there..." The Generals—never mind them not trusting each other, but actually *hating* each other in a lot of cases, all of them in competition for the next star.

Mack: And for press coverage. Who'd get to be in Walter Winchell. Who'd be in Ernie Pyle's.

Scooter: General on General, and here's poor Petoola right in the middle, supposedly in charge of it all, trying to get a unified attack going...

Mack: Hey, he was the worst of what you're talking about. He added to it, did not try to alleviate it at all. You think he wasn't the one chasing the extra star on his shoulder all the time? The only thing Petoola liked better than a fifty-point black ink headline was another medal, another star.

Scooter: That goes without saying, granted. You're a General, you like having a good rep, you like getting appreciated, but I still stay you're being too hard on the guy, a guy with an impossible mission. He tried to save the Abbey, you know.

Mack: That didn't help *us* any. Turns out didn't help the Abbey any either. The two of us used to have this discussion before. I even wrote you once about it. You know what Petoola's biggest problem—his *two* biggest things that made him into the intolerable asshole he was?

Scooter: His middle name and his height. You told me.

Mack: Exactly. His middle name and his looks. First off, what's the name?

Scooter: Wayne, middle name.

Mack: Wayne. Exactly. The fucken guy thinks he's John Wayne out there. It's the O.K. Corral and he's the Duke, walking down Main Street with his posse.

Scooter: That wasn't John Wayne in that.

Mack: Fucken Petoola doesn't even realize that that's the movies and this is war—real war. Doesn't know it's not Montgomery Cliff getting shot out there, it's not William Bendix dying, it's not Richard…who's Richard?…the baby-faced kid, always got his first whisker then got shot at Guadalcanal? You know who I mean? Richard…?

Scooter: Jaeckel.

Mack: Jaeckel. It's not Richard Jaeckel out there, it's us. It's real guys. Fugger doesn't know it's not Hollywood cattle being driven along the Massif, it's mules, real mules.

Scooter: Yeah, I know. How can politicians and movie stars get real war mixed up with the movies, huh? But they do. They do it all the time. Plus, I know, I know, he looks like him too, right? I mean Petoola and John Wayne.

Mack: Exactly. Six-foot something. Big handsome nose on him…

Scooter: Such as your own.

Mack: Well, I don't like to brag, I don't like to blow my own horn, I *do* like to blow my own nose—but fucken Petoola, looking like Randolph Scott every time he gets his mug in the hometown newspaper, in *The New York Times*, *Stars and Stripes*. He's loving it. And we're out there dying by the bucket-full.

***

Petoola and British General Alexander, who was to take charge of the entire operation in southern Italy, shared a powerful, acidic jealousy. Petoola had a good six inches on the little Brit and used it to advantage whenever he could. And history cannot deny Petoola's infatuation with a good publicity shot, any time, anywhere. Left profile. Always the left. The documentation is there.

At Caserta, and again in Naples, he refused to stay in the local palaces that were set up to house the Allied Generals. The HQ, where he and his staff had mapped out the disastrous *Rapido* River crossing, might be a well-furnished farmhouse, but his living quarters had to fit his "Man of the West" image. He let the world know that he—being a simple man, feeling more at home living like an American cowboy, not European royalty—preferred a plain little trailer that had room for only the basic necessities—a bunk, a book, and a bucket of water. As Mack pointed out, he was John Wayne out on a cattle drive, crossing the Red River, not the *Rapido*.

***

Mack: *Rapido* turned red by the time the Krauts got done with us.

***

In Naples Petoola told the press that he felt lost in any big city—Give him the country life any time.

He had been raised in Chicago.

As Mack has also pointed out, he insisted that his name be attached upfront whenever the phrase "Fifth Army" appeared in a newspaper article. It always had to be "General Petoola's Fifth Army."

Getting back to his mediocre mid-career, suddenly at forty-six years old, he became the youngest American Three Star General in our history. Some say his rapid rise from Captain to General had more to do with his nose for good publicity and his friendship with Generals Marshall and Eisenhower than to military acuteness and brilliance.

He was Passenger Number One on a highly secretive submarine journey, to meet with the Vichy forces of France, but he later made sure that the mission was highly reported and covered. After all, Duke Wayne wasn't only a cowboy; in a few movies he was a really good submarine commander too.

Petoola was largely responsible for the decision to go up through Route 6 and over Monte Cassino to get to Rome. He let reporters know early on that it would be a difficult and challenging route, but one that had to be taken, no two ways, it had to be done, and he was the man to do it.

Back in Naples, he set up a photo op of him being given a rare carved stone sculpture from a local Monsignor. He wanted to foster the idea that he was not simply a handsome and brave American cowboy, but also a true lover of the arts. A preserver of Western Culture. This image got a bit nicked when it came time for him to destroy the Monastery at Monte Cassino, but more on that later.

As the war in southern Italy schleped on, his fears would grow to almost paranoiac proportions, especially when he felt that other countries and other personalities would receive the credit for *his* glory, *his* march to Rome.

He harbored a strong dislike not just for Alexander, for all of his British counterparts; he saw them as rivals for newspaper space. They were "feather-dusters" and "peanuts" who could rob him of his beloved headlines. He held a particular distaste for British General Monte, who had one-upped Petoola with the front page photo of Monte reaching *down* from the back of a truck to shake Petoola's hand. Monte's nose for news—news about himself—was as grand as Petoola's, and Monte hated the perception that he was playing second banana to the Yank here in Italy. After all, he had been the darling of North Africa, right?

Petoola recognized a dangerous rival when he saw one, and he assembled a crew of no fewer than fifty public relations men on his staff. Fifty guys who could stay out of harm's way in those smelly trenches, as long as they slavishly adhered to the boss's rules. His "Three-to-one rule" spelled out that Petoola's name had to appear no fewer than three times on the first page of any story, then at least once a page from there on in to the final -30-.

He would have loved the pages you're now reading.

***

Scooter: Maybe not.

***

He went so far as to personally hire some ad men of the New York City advertising agencies to advise him on public relations and image building. He insisted that every segment of "his" army had its own P.R. department. One unsuspecting G.I. name of Jack was happily digging latrines one day when Petoola's men approached him, then checked to find out if Jack had really been a newspaperman in civilian life, and then rescued Jack from a career in the disposing of shit in favor of a career in the slinging of it. Jack learned to type "With General Petoola's Fifth Army Front in Italy" faster than he could type his own name, and he began every story with that phrase. There would be hell to pay if he didn't.

Each conquered city was a notch on the handle of Petoola's six-shooter reputation. He sent his wife the city of Naples as a "birthday present." In Rome he had the huge city sign sent back home as a keepsake.

Yes, he only allowed himself to be photographed from the left side, his "good side." As somebody once said: "War is the purest form of publicity by other means."

***

Mack: He should've gone to Hollywood for his publicity, instead of off to war.
Scooter: I still say you guys are being too hard on the guy. It's not so much being vane, it's having self-confidence. There's never

been a General who hasn't had a uniform full of bluster, right underneath that chest full of medals.

Mack: Not Eisenhower.

Scooter: Maybe not. But maybe he was just better at camouflaging it, huh?

Mack: No, Ike truly was aware of the enlisted man. I remember Terry telling me—you remember Terry? Drove a transport? One day he's in North Africa, they're having a game of pinochle, they look up, Ike's standing there. Ike himself. He sits down, actually plays a few hands. There's no reporters around, no photographers, Ike's just relaxing with his men.

Scooter: That's pretty good.

Mack: Wait. Terry's outfit gets shipped out, they land at Salerno, trudge their way up Italy, like we did, then the poor guy's up in England, lands at Normandy, finally gets to slog across Europe, finally, it's the end, he's back in England, he's getting a metal pinned on him by…by who? Who you think?

Scooter: Ike.

Mack: Ike. Hasn't seen the dogface since years before, North Africa, and Ike says to him now, "So how's the pinochle game going?" You would've though Ike had a few other things on his mind in the interim. But there he is, remembering some dogface he played pinochle with in North Africa for a half-hour. You think Petoola would've done that? He was too busy screwing up campaigns, getting his troops butchered, getting his mug in the newspaper, checking out how his hair's parted in the mirror.

***

Horrible and mass-grave-deadly errors were made throughout the Italian campaign.

The first was that decision to push up Route 6 all the way to Rome. Petoola's army had just fought its way through the mountains down at the tip of Italy, so he envisioned a clear, relatively flat, relatively easy road from there on up. Tanks, tanks, tanks. Maybe get a couple Movietone News shots of him sticking his head up through the gun turret. The *Liri* Valley, with its watchtower-like Monastery above, did not seem to pose much of an obstacle. That of course was Error Number One.

In the big picture, Petoola felt that the war, especially the part of it here in southern Italy, could be won on the roads and in the air, with the Allies' superior mechanization and air power. Another error. A victory would actually require thousands of foot soldiers squirming on their bellies in pain in mud-filled trenches and fields. The good old fashioned way to win a war. The Frenchman Juin, we've seen, could not convince this American ersatz-cowboy that the Monte Cassino route was not the way to get to Roma, that the best course was to use strategy and maneuvering rather than mechanized force which—when driving across muck and up the steep sides of a mountain—was no force at all.

***

Scooter: Remember, Petoola was under a lot of pressure from Washington and Churchill to get moving, to bust on through and get up to Rome. He kept insisting he could do it, and that led to some impetuous decision making.

Mack: Yeah, like the *Rapido*.

***

Guys who knew the score, and could see a few moves into the future, guys like General Tuker of the Indian Division, tried to paint a picture for Petoola, tried to make him see what a senseless bloodbath a frontal assault on the valley and the hills around Monte Cassino would be, but Tuker's words and ideas just fell unheeded on those big, floppy, Texas Panhandle ears of Petoola's.

All of these pressures and voices had led to the Battle at the *Rapido*, below those leering eyes of the Monetary on the hill—eyes that were gazing down, seeing all, like the billboard eyes of Dr. T. J. Eckleberg in the Gatsby story, except in this case the Americans thought it was Nazi eyes staring out of the hundred portals of the Abbey, with Nazi hands scratching down latitudes and longitudes in their pads to pass on to their boys in the artillery units.

Petoola's fellow American General, Fred Walker, knew going in that it would be a senseless slaughter. Over a thousand American boys were turned into mule meat during that first horrible night on the *Rapido*, and then Petoola takes a deep breath, a Gary Cooper breath, and tells the poor fools to head back in the next morning, in a sunlit suicide ballet. Well, it would have been suicide if Petoola had gone along with them.

After it was all done, and the bodies had been hauled off—it was, *Well then, blame the British.* Blame the powder puff Brits. The British commander had actually come to the Yanks to apologize for their failure to get across and set up a diversion and grab some high ground. The Americans were told that an attack was now foolish, impossible. Petoola went ahead with the attack. He felt that the Brits were being too dependent on aerial bombardment and on artillery. He believed that a full frontal infantry attack would show the Brits how things got done.

Scorecards simply reduce the human lives to statistics—make the men into mules—but here it is again anyway: in the Battle at the *Rapido*, four hundred and thirty American were killed attempting to cross the river, nine hundred dead or wounded who never even got to the river. There were seven hundred seventy American troops captured. The Germans lost but sixty-four men. That's not a victory of attrition, that's not a victory at all.

Nothing had been gained by the attack. Petoola's Fifth Army was in the same position, worse, than before.

It takes a lot for the typical American enlisted man to get fed up. He'll complain and curse from the moment he steps off the bus in Basic, but then he'll put up with almost any absurd and bloody plan. Yet, after the war, those men of the 36th demanded that Congressional investigation into this horror. The men's testimony described the teary-eyed officers as their men marched off into the meat grinder.

***

Scooter: Petoola was exonerated.

Mack: I am not impressed.

***

A New Zealand officer said that nothing was right about the attack in its planning and action, nothing except one thing: the courage shown by the men who died.

After the failure to cross the *Liri* Valley by an amphibious crossing of the *Rapido*, attention now turned again to the Abbey on the hill. That might have been a good time to reconsider things—reconsider Juen's plan to use the mountains, reconsider the Anzio landing, reconsider the entire "Soft Underbelly" plan and instead ship out to England to get ready for the D-Day invasion.

Juen had no respect for Petoola. At various times during the campaign, Petoola would give him impossible orders—orders to transport supplies through the worst and most fortified trails of the mountains. So many mules had been killed that Juen's men sometimes had to transport using only their feet and backs, heading out on trips that were eight hours long, filled with death coming down from above and danger up from below. Juen's men thought that Petoola's orders were "Mad." They followed them anyway.

American Generals also had their problems with Petoola. Omar Bradley thought he was "False, too eager to impress and get promoted." Patton saw him as too damn slick, preferring self-promotion over victory.

But by then there was simply too much egg smeared across the faces of the military leaders in southern Italy to do an About

Face. Suppose the newspapers started playing up the "What the hell's going on down there" angle? On the battle maps—maps that could be posted up on the front pages of major metropolitan dailies—the black arrows made it look like a simple step. We had the air power, we had the tanks, we had the artillery, we had the man power, why the hell weren't we pushing forward?

"It's the Abbey," was the answer; that was the excuse they came up with. "It's that damned Monastery on the hill." In this case the "damned" was a perfect and multi-layered use of the word.

***

Scooter: Again, in Petoola's defense, he was against the destruction of the Abbey at first.

***

But the ultimate decision of whether to destroy the Monastery or not rested on those broad cowboy shoulders. He had people whispering into both his broad cowboy ears; the choice would be his.

You could guess that little Juin-bug was against the destruction. His brilliant military sense and foresight made him realize that the reduction of the holy place into rubble would achieve nothing, and might even offer the Germans better defensive positions while also giving them a propaganda weapon.

But as you know, Petoola had little affection and no respect for the Frenchman.

As Petoola's one ear was being assailed by the French accent, his other ear was hearing Kiwi. The leader of the New Zealand troops, General Freyberg, was saying that the Monastery had to go. This voice held some power; Freyberg was the one leader in that country who could personally decide to remove his troops from the fray if he so desired. And remember, less than half of Petoola's troops were American. He could not afford to lose an alley.

Most of the American Generals were against the idea of destroying the Abbey. Aerial photography had revealed no German personal or weaponry inside the building.

Italian peasants interviewed by American intelligence said that there were only helpless peasants and religious monks there. Mules.

But Petoola's own mules—his fighting men—saw the Abbey on the hill as the killing eyes of the German army.

***

Scooter: Yes. We all wanted the place blasted to bits. We have to admit that much, huh, Mack?
Mack: Sure. Of course we did.

***

Meanwhile, Petoola's massive ego also came into play on the other side. He did not wish to be seen by the world as a barbaric conqueror. He would constantly have his Press Corps issue statements that no church, no holy place would be destroyed by the Allies unless there was direct proof that it was being used by the enemy for military purposes.

Months later he would cringe at a Roman dinner party when an Italian lady of leisure was introduced to him and said, "So you're the second barbarian to conquer Rome." Belasarius, 536 A.D., being the first. Petoola didn't like the company—not Belasarius, and certainly not this dame who was standing there after he had freed her country, now calling him a barbarian.

***

Scooter: Didn't John Wayne knock out Susan Hayworth with one punch in some movie?

***

Petoola arranged to have dinner with a high-ranking American chaplain and made sure that the chaplain would bring back one clear message to Cardinal Spellman in New York City—the good General Petoola was dead set against the destruction of the Monastery at Monte Cassino. Spellman was the most powerful and visible of American Cardinals, the Top Gun of Roman Catholics America, and Petoola didn't want to get on this guy's bad side.

But, counter-balancing all of that was the American press and the American high command, asking: "What's going on? Why aren't you moving forward? Look at the map. Those pretty arrows are stagnating. What—it's because of a church that you're stuck in the mud? One damned church? Our boys are dying over there." Even the nearly-sanctified Eisenhower was saying that when it comes down to either some artwork or American lives, we save the lives. Every time.

Petoola, trying to get this five hundred ton monkey off his back, tried for the "If you tell me to do it, I'll do it," approach.

In the end, somebody told him to do it.

In the end, he did it.

And so it had come time to turn the Monastery into a mule.

It would have to be destroyed.

***

Chapter Seven:
Destruction of a Monastery

"And there, uplifted, like a passing cloud
That pauses on a mountain summit high,
Monte Cassino's convent rears its proud
And venerable walls against the sky.
…in my convent cell,
Myself not yet myself, in dreams I lay,
And, as a monk who hears the matin bell,
Started from sleep;—already it was day."

-from "Monte Cassino" by Henry Wadsworth Longfellow 1875
***

On February 15, 1944, one sunrise after Saint Valentine's Day—that day when tokens of affection and love are given and received—Saint Benedict's prediction was finally and fully realized, as his monastery was blown to shit. His home, Sis Scholastica's home, home to his order of monks for fourteen centuries, home to the greatest art and cultural treasures of the Western world—was destroyed for the fourth time. That earthbound fortress built to withstand the forces of Satan was no match for the Flying Fortresses built to destroy the house of enemies, and over a four hour period, first the American B-17 Flying Fortresses, then the twin-engined Mitchell war planes, then the sloppy seconds Marauders, all took turns at obliterating the building—reducing it and its contents to a steaming pile of once-glorious rubble.

You're reading a book right now, but what you probably want to do is watch the videos of the bombing of the Monte Carlo Monastery. My word-slinging skills are okay, on a good day, and those of Mathew Parker and David Hapgood and David Richardson (those guys who wrote the *factual* books about Monte Cassino) are excellent, but nobody's words—black and white smudges on paper—can compare with the black and white pixels that move and dart across your eyes on the screen.

So what you do is: Go to YouTube, punch in "Battle of Monte Cassino," and observe. Use the full-screen view. There are many clips to choose from, but at least take a look at "A Soldiers Story" and the stuff from the 20th Century's War Channel. Some of the web addresses to use are: Youtube.com/watch?v=kSEOY-3D=Zo and YouTube.com/watch7v=G14UNe7cMOg. I think. The videos are as black and white as this page, but you'll come away feeling that nothing about this attack was clear cut, nothing was neat or comprehensible.

Some of the sound tracks are in foreign languages—Polish, Italian—it won't matter. You'll know exactly what is being said, and that is not the important thing anyhow. Just words. A few clips have some hokey music playing, also not needed. Tunes. You'll know what you are feeling; the images may burn into your sight and stay there awhile. Emotion. Check it out.

In the meantime, allow me and Scooter and Mack to give you our half-assed and pissed-off view of this thing that happened more than half a century ago.

***

The Lead-up

The leader of the New Zealand troops in Italy, General Freyberg, was the most outspoken voice lobbying for the bombing of the Abbey. His feelings could be easily understood, since his Kiwis and their Maoris Polynesian compatriots would lose more men per capita than any other Allied country; he would blame a lot of those losses on that damn German-occupied fortress sitting above them at the top of the hill.

Petoola was still arguing that a well laid-out second infantry attack on the Valley—together with Freyberg's well-rested and always-disciplined troops, coordinated with the wild, shaved-head Gurkhas from India and other internationals—could take the area, despite the Monastery's placement and its strategic value. Petoola was resentful that these "British" troops—as he saw them all—would be grabbing the glory that he had missed out on with his *Rapido* fiasco, but still, he was the guy in charge and getting his multinational army back into gear heading north would powder up his image nicely. His blemishes were showing, the world was watching, he had to get it right this time—but his bottom line remained: We do it with mass infantry, not by bombing the Monastery.

Freyberg took a beady-eyed look at the same situation and insisted, "We're not going anywhere unless you get rid of that bloody Abbey on the hill."

Italian museum authorities ("You cannot destroy the art within"), Papal Representatives ("It is sacred ground"), Eisenhower ("We don't destroy churches unless absolutely necessary"), and the Frenchman Juin ("Use the mountains, you imbecile, go around the Valley, through the mountains"), and the Germans ("We're not in there anyway"), all put their weight on the other side—the side of preservation of the sacred building.

Fly-bys and reconnaissance seemed to back up the Germans' claims that they were respecting the Monastery's neutrality. Frido swore that his troops were honoring the three hundred meter free zone around the Monastery and, for the most part, they were. Yet people see what they want to—especially when they are being drilled by stress and by bullets—and so there were various Allied reports of uniformed Germans entering and occupying the building.

When examined closely, especially in the luxury of peacetime hindsight, these reports held no credence, but what *did* hold credence, rock-hard tons and tons of credence, was a page from a Naples library book, printed 1879, which described the impregnable structure of the eventual target. The Monastery was a massive building, built to keep out the devil and the world, a building perfectly suited for keeping out any invader, either from this world or beyond. The building had only one entrance, in front, consisting of huge timbers and massive stones, with no cracks in the walls where enemy soldiers or venial sins could gain entry. The single entrance was sealed and guarded by huge brass doors. Above the doors, seeming to rest there undisturbed in quiet confidence, was the word "Pax."

Each Abbey wall climbed to a height of one hundred fifty feet, and was ten foot wide at the base. No weapon built in the centuries before this one could have penetrated this holy fortress. Even the modern heavy bombs of 1944 would have to be delivered in mass quantities in order to put a dent into what Saint Benedict had wrought.

Many military strategists, including the U.S. General Keys, knew the building and knew how wars were fought; they pointed out that bombing the place would actually turn it in to a *better* defensive site for the Germans, offering nooks to hide in and crannies to shoot from.

Plus…a gaggle of innocent monks and refugees was living there.

A U.S. Air Corps General took all this into consideration, then bragged to his superiors that his planes could rip the building out of the mountaintop like a dentist ripping out a dead tooth.

"But you can't flatten an entire mountain."

"We can sure as hell try."

What finally determined the decision to annihilate the Abbey was more psychological than strategic. Any fighting man looking up that steep hill at the silent building had to imagine those multiple windows as eyes—watching, waiting, almost narrowing with a grin. Eyes that were seeing all, controlling all; making all those huddled below feel naked and unprotected. Those Dr. T. J. Eckleberg eyes again, but with rockets.

In the days following the brutality against the Abbey, everyone seemed to scramble away from the title of "The One Who Called It In," but in the end it would have to have been Petoola who gave the go-ahead. The Monastery would have to be destroyed.

***

Powerful snowstorms had hit the area two days before, but the weather for February 15th was predicted to be clear. Clear enough for the pilots and navigators and bombardiers to locate their target, clear enough for those on the ground to witness the event—an event that was designed for media as much as militia.

On the day before the scheduled bombing, Valentine's Day, leaflets were dropped like snow over the Monastery, warning inhabitants that the time had come—come and gone—that the bones of Saint Benedict were about to be blasted. The leaflets were written in Italian and English; let the Germans translate for themselves.

A peasant boy walking the grounds outside the walls picked up one of the leaflets and brought it in to show to the monks and to the refugees. They all just pursed their lips and shook their disbelieving *paisan* heads: This is an American bluff, something like this could never happen. This is the Abbey of Saint Benedict.

***

For the mission to have any semblance of military relevance at all, the bombing would have to be immediately followed by the ground attack of Freyberg's New Zealanders, along with the Indian and international troops. But when the "Destroy" command was given, nobody bothered to check to see if these troops were in position to attack.

They weren't.

Indians and Kiwis had been sent up the Massif to replace the exhausted or dead Americans, but these reinforcements were so hampered by the mud and rain and the loss of so many mules that they would not be in position to attack after the bombing. When the reinforcements finally did get up the mountain, they found the Americans in such a sorry state that they had to be carried out on stretchers. Or in body bags.

No one was ready.

No one bothered to check.

The bombers would take off as scheduled.

***

The Bomber Crews

Powdered eggs. Every fucken morning, the same fucken powdered eggs. Life for the bomb crews of southern Italy in between missions was dull, boring, a surrealistic loop-tape. If you haven't—or even if you have—go read Joe Heller's *Catch-22*. He was there. As you read about Yossarian and his crew, remember that the truth is always more absurd than fiction.

Farting out their egg methane, the crews of the Foggia Air Field near Naples ambled out of the mess hall and assembled for their preflight briefing. Boys, today's mission ought to be a short one. And a sweet one. And photogenic too. You might even get on the news.

The crews were told that the Krauts and the Ey-ties were taking advantage of our decent and humane decision not to bomb churches, mosques and hospitals. Those sons of bitches were infesting some ancient Monastery up north that none of the fliers had ever heard of, bloating the place full with heavy artillery and observation posts. We'll have to put an end to that. No one mentioned but everyone knew that other churches, mosques and hospitals had often been bombed, and would be again.

Schools, orphanages, places of worship—never mind all that, here's the good part: this place offers a perfect target; a bombardier with two glass eyes couldn't miss this place if he was drunk, asleep and catatonic. Picture the hill as one perfectly formed tit, then the church as a perfect nipple. How many of you guys would have trouble finding a nice nipple atop a nice tit? Right?

Some fliers remember being told that if they had religious scruples against hitting the place—Catholic—then they could sit this one out. Most did not remember being told that; it would not have mattered anyway. This would be one more deployment mission to be tallied, and a freebie; one more step toward getting back home. An easy step too, easier than risking antiaircraft fire all the way up to Rome and back. The only reservations the fliers felt came from the fact that American troops were camped very close to the target. Nobody likes killing their own guys; it happens, but you don't have to like it.

A single Flying Fortress—just one B-17 with four engines, carrying twelve five hundred pound demolition bombs—could reek incredible havoc on a site, could cause unimaginable destruction on the ground. The plane was loud and powerful, and its load was deadly. That February day, not just one or two but an incredible amount of the bombers—thirty-seven of them—would fly up to bomb Cassino. On their way they would be joined by more bombers, from other basses. Surely not thirty-seven more? Surely the Foggia squadron had to be the biggest. In fact, *one hundred and seven more* B-17's would be part of the attack. Each carrying those twelve five hundred pound bombs. Then the B-17's would be followed eighty-six medium bombers. Don't even bother doing the math. After the initial B-17's, forty-seven of those twin engine Mitchells, and then forty-one Marauders, would finish the job. Kill and re-kill the overkill.

Petoola had said all along that he did not want to bomb the Monastery, but if he did it, he was going to do it right. The attack was comprised of the most bombers ever sent against a single target. Even the Kiwi hawk, Freyberg, had only asked for thirty-six fighter-bombers to do the job. No one has been able to ascertain why the attack had grown so out of proportion to the target—a single building.

***

Mack: That was Petoola, putting on an air show for the cameras. He knew what it would look like back home. Would screen up real nice.

***

Evidence doesn't support that. Petoola actually didn't even have authorization to determine what planes or how many would be used. He wasn't even present at the site on the day.

***

Mack: Doesn't matter. It was him.

***

The number painted on the side and the tail of the lead bomber could not have been more prophetic: Six-sixty-six. The Devil's number.

***

Scooter: Who's writing this script?
Mack: The devil destroys the church.

***

So Bomber 666 and the rest of its squadron flew up the coast and had no trouble spotting the target. It was a clear day and the Monastery walls looked nearly pure white atop the hill. The lead plane's bombardier was one of the most accurate around (no Yossarian he); he leaned over his glowing Pilot Directional Indicator and then he let loose.

Like hundreds of giant dark birds shitting as they flew, the bombers did their job quickly and efficiently; they then banked around for the return flight home. Few if any of the aircrews knew that their payloads were splattering an indelible mark on the pages of history.

***

The Innocents: The Peasants

After that Italian peasant kid who had been walking outside the Abbey found one of the warning leaflets dropped by the Americans and then brought it inside to Abbot Gregorio Diamare, a German office was shown the leaflet. He told the monks that it was just more piece of American propaganda, *scheiss*, fear tactics, no one would ever destroy this holy place. But they all know who God helps, so it was decided that the peasants would be evacuated the next morning.

Their white flag could be interpreted as laundry, and many of them could be slaughtered on the road—the fighting had become that intense and that indiscriminant. If some of them would venture off the mule path, the Germans would shoot them as spies. Some peasants figured that they had been tricked into leaving because the monks needed what was left of the food for themselves.

Some of the peasants left the morning of the bombing, but some, maybe eight hundred, stayed. Some estimates say as many as a thousand remained.

Weeks before there had been an earlier evacuation of the peasants—all but those too sick to leave—but the combination of a violent thunderstorm and especially heavy artillery fire had caused a group of them to leave the caves in which they had been hiding and to return to pound on the door of the Monastery. The monks had been instructed in the Corporal Works of Mercy, but more importantly, the peasants were threatening to set fire to their beloved front door, so the visitors were allowed reentry.

***

Mack: What year was it the fans used a battering ram to bust down a gate at Ebbets Field, got in to see the World Series? 1924? Yeah, 1924.

Scooter: What? You're talking about…?

Mack: Same thing.

Scooter: What?

Mack: Bedford Avenue. Flatbush. Smashing in the gate to get in. Just like the peasants.

Scooter: What?

***

Unlike the soldiers on both sides, the peasants had always looked upon the Monastery as a hub of sanctity, of holiness, a refuge from the horrors of the world.

Before the war came, if a peasant ever began doubting the existence of God, he could raise his eyes up to that white edifice against the sky above him, and he would see the Power first hand. God is our Monastery. The mountains are His arms and His hands, holding us, protecting us.

The neighborhood kids were more worldly than that, and they would play "Attack the Fort" and "King of the Hill," using sticks for guns and rocks for grenades, scampering around the fields and hills below.

But now, whether they were still inside the building or huddled in a nearby cave, each peasant was cold, hungry, sick, scared—not overly consumed with the joy of being one of Christ's children.

Things had become so bad that they held a common belief that things could get no worse.

Then dysentery had brought its "jerky restlessness of death" to them and to their children.

Then typhoid fever had swept through their ranks like a tidal wave.

Then the bombers came.

***

The Innocents II: The Monks

Martino Matronola was the Abbot Diamare's secretary and chief assistant, a "go-to" guy who could speak German and work the street, both sides of it, as well as up above and maybe even the sewers below. He met now with a German officer to discuss evacuating the peasants; then he returned to the Abbot and the other monks who were refusing to leave their spiritual and material home. For these men of God, the borderline between life and after-life was more blurred than it is for us secular souls, so the decision for the monks to remain was an easy one. Fifty-five of them did.

At 8:30 on the morning of the bombing, the holy men gathered in a small makeshift chapel in the northwest corner of the Monastery; there they recited their devotions. They prayed to a statue of the Madonna that they had hauled over from Saint Benedict's tomb. Then they proceeded in a solemn line to the room of their elderly and feeble Abbot, so that they all could pray, and maybe die, as one.

Their beloved Abbot gave each one of his monks Absolution for his sins, preparing their souls for meeting God. The only words that had been spoken for hours had been whispered words of prayer.

A strange distant rumble was heard far off. The sound was growing nearer, growing louder, meaner.

The monks were on their knees when 666's first bomb hit.

***

The Witnesses

Show time in the Valley.

Allied soldiers had been given the day off on February 15, a holiday. They weren't told exactly why, but speculation, rumor and gossip managed to figure it out. Crowds of gawkers gathered on Monte Trocchio, a spot across the Valley which offered the best view of Monte Cassino. Reporters both civilian and with *Stars and Stripes* opened their notebooks and aimed their cameras; they scribbled and clicked. The troops were to read later in *Newsweek* that this was "the most advertised single bombing in history."

***

Mack: I didn't know you advertised a bombing. Beer, lunchmeat, Chryslers, Philcos, those you advertise, but bombings?

Scooter: We were excited.

Mack: Yes, indeed. Everybody was. I'd never seen a crowd that whipped up since I was standing in the bleachers, Yankee Stadium, Harland Svare, Giants' left-side linebacker, intercepted a pass, ran it back eighty yards.

Scooter: This was different.

Mack: Who was that against? The Steelers maybe, Bobby Lane? If it was, some receiver would've gotten his ass chewed. Little Bobby, no facemask—they were for sissies—sticking that mug right into some split-end's face, cursing him out, telling him to run the god-damn pattern, for Christ sake.

Scooter: This was different. We saw that black smoke billowing up, engulfing the place, the place was disappeared, then the smoke and dust settles, blows away, there's whole pieces of the walls gone, just crumbled, so fast. Then, more planes, more smoke and dust, the whole thing happens all over again, and a whole new cheer goes up, even louder. Louder every time it happens. Somebody was yelling, "Touchdown," every time, remember? Guys throwing up their two arms like refs with a field goal.

Mack: We were all hoarse by then, just yelling our throats raw.

Scooter: I stopped yelling after a couple more hits. Maybe halfway through. I just got still. Got a little water in my eyes even. I don't know why, I figured it was a very good thing happening. But still…

Mack: Me too, I guess. A little bit.

Scooter: I'm still not sure why.

***

The bombs fell like a string of black turds and it took a moment for the black smashing smoke to rise up and engulf the Monastery. The black mixed with the white of the walls blowing apart. And red, there was red—red bolts of fire. That doesn't show up on the old, grainy movies of the event. But the photography is pretty good. Magazine still cameras along with movie cameras had been set up and focused in from over on Monte Trocchio.

***

Mack: It took what seemed like a whole minute for the sound to reach us, remember? It's like when you see a guy using a sledge hammer. You think you're standing close, but the sound's never in rhythm with the hammer hitting. We were close, as close as anyone, except maybe the Gurkhas and the Zealanders up there, but still, the sound didn't coordinate.

Scooter: We were close enough.

***

The Abbey's steeple and then the cupola tipped and disappeared, like goalposts after a hometown victory.

Petoola had stayed home at Presenzano, his headquarters, miles away, did not attend.

***

Mack: In case it got bad ink.

***

Ironically, some stray bombs from the attack actually fell close behind his headquarters.

***

Mack: Serves the bastard right.

***

In the German war room, windows rattled and the walls vibrated. The aides to German General Frido vonSenger had never heard a noise anything like this. They turned to the General. He knew what was happening; he just shook his head. "The idiots." He drove to a spot about five miles away from the bombing and from there he watched the fire show. "The idiots."

When all the planes had disappeared, Frido still stood and watched. He knew that his military position had not been weakened by the onslaught. None of his men had been in the building.

***

The soldiers of the Indian Division were supposed to be ready for an assault directly after the bombing. They were shocked by the event and for a few moments had no idea what was going on. *Newsweek* had been told, *Stars and Stripes* had been alerted. Officers and nurses had come all the way up from Naples, packing sandwiches, to witness the event. But nobody had bothered to tell the Indians. They were very near to the destruction, but nowhere near ready for any follow-up attack. Nobody had bothered to tell them.

They had fought their way up the Snake's Head as best they could, attempting to be in proper position for a post-bombing attack, but it had been an impossible task. The crucial Point 593 was still in German control, despite what they had been told. They had been clobbered by Nebelwerfers, six-barreled mortars, by Screaming Meemies. Their medical supplies had run out and some of the wounded had died while trying to self-apply tourniquets of barbed wire, anything to stem the bleeding. They had fought Germans hand-to-hand in complete darkness, like something out of a Genghis Khan nightmare. Now they were neither in condition nor in position for an attack.

So they settled back in the mud and, like everybody else, watched the air show.

The monks who had remained in the Abbey gripped their rosary beads and felt the shivering shoulders of fellow monks pressing up against theirs as the Abbot continued to dispense the sacrament of Absolution. Their souls were approaching the entrance to the Kingdom of Heaven. Chunks of cement and chunks of metal would fly through the air. Something collapsed around them…a wall?...a ceiling?...and they knew they had become entombed. None of the monks cried out, but all of them could hear the peasants screaming from somewhere. The men of God knelt together in prayer as they felt and heard their beloved Monastery crumbling around them. Could heaven ever be as beautiful as this condemned place had been? They began to sing a hymn to the Blessed Virgin.

A deaf-mute monk ran to them from the blasted-out basilica; he was in a panic, somehow he had missed what was going on. He clutched a religious metal to his chest and tried to ask for an explanation. The sudden bombing must have been even worse for him, not being able to hear each deafening explosion, but to merely feel it in the walls and in his bones. In heaven his hearing and his voice would be restored. His fellow monks had been stuffing their ears with scrapes of material, hoping to become as deaf as he was.

The Italian young man who had brought the warning leaflets in to the monks was huddled with his family in a fairly secure section of the building. But when the noise and the impact drove him to panic, he ran outside to escape. Out there on the mule path, where German soldiers trained their machineguns on him until he returned to the dying building.

Some refugees went crazy and ran out, trying to catch a bomb as it hit and exploded.

Some were led to the cell of Saint Benedict. They were told that they would be safe there, that the bombs could not hurt them there. It was true. Saint Benedict's cell somehow remained untouched by the bombing—the hand of God or just a quirk of physics, didn't matter.

Outside, the side of the mountain was on fire. The flames on the olive trees and the scrub brush would burn for a week.

The media strained to find the right words to describe what they were witnessing. The BBC's Chris Buckley reported that the planes flew "in perfect formation with that arrogant dignity" that only bomber aircraft can achieve. He reported that the side of the mountain quickly bust into huge flames, as if a giant had scraped a huge match across its face.

The New York Times was more prosaic and called the event "the worst aerial and artillery onslaught ever directed against a single building."

***

The Reactions

Scooter: If Vonnegut had been in that basement, he would've had a prequel to *Slaughterhouse 5*.

Mack: *Slaughterhouse 4*?

***

The Vatican announced that it was horrified by the destruction. Washington and London swallowed hard, feeling guilty but assured—now things could get moving. No one in the Allied Chain of Command would assume responsibility for calling in the bombs. The closest anyone came was a lowly Captain who admitted passing the word that no less than FDR and Churchill were demanding the place be bombed and bombed good.

The Germans realized they had just been awarded two prizes: a propaganda bonanza and an area that could be more easily fortified. Their spirit and their will to resist had been strengthened by the attack.

It had taken only a few hours (along with two hundred and fifty-three tons of bombs) to destroy centuries of culture, art and piety.

The monks' faces were ghostly white now, bleached by the cement dust and by fear, but they were not ghosts. They had survived. They dug their way out of the rubble and proceeded to tearfully examine the damage. Most of their Monastery was unrecognizable. A giant steaming crater had replaced the central courtyard. The basilica, the sacristy, the other courtyards, had all been smashed into dust. Frescoes and painting were gone, simply gone. Dust and smoke were twirling through the air like rotted incense. The entire roof of the basilica had been blown off, pulverized.

The statue of Saint Benedict had survived, but it had been decapitated. It was now as brainless as the attack had been.

All the monks had survived, but the peasants had not. First they had huddled together in the cellar of the *collegio*, part of that

Disneyworld-like alternate universe thirty feet below ground. Those who had been told to go to Saint Benedict's cell did, and they were saved. Some did not and were not. Mothers clutched their rosary beads and their babies. Wailing and praying echoed off the walls and had mixed with the sound of the Armageddon explosions. If your body was not to be destroyed that day, your mind would be. No one's sanity could survive this.

Of the two hundred and thirty innocent peasants killed in the Abbey that long winter, estimates say about half of them died in those few hours of bombing. One hundred and forty-eight skulls were found in the smoking ruins. Someone had been assigned the task of counting skulls.

To the monks it was a hundred fewer mouths to feed and bellies to fill. The dead were with the Lord now. At rest. Joyful. Fulfilled at last.

Those peasants who had survived had been blasted into a state of semi-consciousness; their faces as dull and emotionless as their screams had been just awhile before. Some of them were fleeing the Monastery. Too late. Fleeing from what? To where? Many of the survivors were children, most of them orphaned or abandoned, all the peasants were delirious. Some tried to get away from the ruins; others tried to get back in.

The Gates of Heaven had been closed. The gate of the Monastery had been annihilated by munitions.

Matronola wrote out a statement in German, and the ancient and shaken Abbot Diamare signed it: It stated that no Germans had been in the Monastery.

Actually that was not true; there had been one. A German soldier had defected with a letter personally signed by Pius XII, directing any bishop to ordain this young German as a priest. The Abbot had readily agreed. "Before I die," he said, "I will give God one more priest." He never got the chance.

Other than this young pious priest wannabe, there was not a single German in the Monastery.

As the "Pax" sign above the door had advertised, the building had remained a place of peace to the very end.

The Procession

As far as I know, Sam Peckinpah and Federico Fellini never collaborated on a movie. If they had, the script could have come from a scene on the Monte Cassino Massif following the bombing. Dante could have done the screenplay.

Amidst an atmosphere of complete silent, movement was seen within the ruins. An informal truce had been declared and soldiers from both sides now studied this movement.

A crucifix appeared. Then a slow, orderly profession of surviving monks, maybe twelve, maybe forty, each with the face hidden within a black caul, followed the crucifix and followed their Abbot down the mule paths. As the procession twisted and descended its way over the chunks of broken rock and steaming granite, the Rosary was recited.

The monks looked absurdly young and innocent. A few were carrying their suitcases. The procession continued silently down, following the mule trail, down through Dante's Inferno. Some dying peasants were being carried on ladders acting as stretchers.

The procession was fired upon.

A woman was being carried on one of the improvised stretcher because she had lost her feet in the bombing; she was abandoned there.

One old monk had not joined the procession; he had chosen to remain in the ruins of the Monastery to await his death. He was one of the fortunate ones.

***

Total Allied Military Gains Achieved by the Bombing

None.

***

Chapter Eight:
The Art Lovers Caravan

"The Angelic Doctor as a school-boy played,
And dreamed perhaps the dreams, that he repeats
In ponderous folios for scholastics made."

-from "Monte Cassino" by Henry Wadsworth Longfellow 1875

***

Months before the bombing, there had been another procession out of the Monastery, but this one had been more frantic and focused. Because of this earlier trip down the mountainside, many of the art and religious treasures that it had held were saved when the Monastery at Monte Cassino was destroyed.

They were saved by a doctor and a Nazi.

The doctor was Max Becker, a tall, good looking guy who had grown up in Germany with dual citizenship; his mother was

English, his father German. This duality wasn't an invitation to high status as the Nazis came to power in the late thirties; a gang of guys wearing brown shirts and sullen looks had beaten him unconscious in the streets of his hometown. He realized that time was running short if he wished to leave the Fatherland before things got even worse for half-breeds like him and breeds in general. With only one semester left in medical school, Max applied for a transfer to the University of Edinburgh, kilts instead of jodhpurs. The U. of Ed told him that they would not accept his German credits so, rather than starting back at the beginning of his medical studies, he decided to stay in Germany just until graduation.

Bad move. Things heated up fast, ethical barriers grew horns even faster, the Blitzkrieg started blitzing, and Hitler's army could always use a few more good doctors—so at the age of thirty-three Max found himself in the German army with a responsibility and a secret. Luckily for Dr. Max, he wasn't sent to the Russia Front, but instead was assigned to run a military aid station in southern Italy, where his love of art and culture—along with his ability to see what lay ahead—would come into play.

Max knew that the Allies would eventually push their way up from Sicily to the north, and that this warfront would mean destruction—including a mass destruction of irreplaceable art. Unlike most Germans—unlike most people—he acted on his concerns for the world. He finagled, pled, ducked 'n' weaved, and he learned to use what the Italians refer to as *"frigatura"*—that sort of activity that isn't quite illegal or legal, but very common, bending rules to the point where they almost break but don't—and he managed get most of the treasures of the national library of Naples hidden away and out of harm's way before that city was shattered by the war.

Now, he felt he had to do the same for Monte Cassino. Maybe the peasants saw God on that hill as they looked up at the Monastery, but Dr. Max saw culture and civilization up there, residing within those thick but brittle walls.

He was a medical man with no authority for this type of undertaking—no experience, no knowledge or skill, but the rescue filled him with a sense of accomplishment rivaled only by his sense of duty of saving lives during this hellish period in his country's history.

As the Allies crept closer to Monte Cassino, young Dr. Max knew what needed to be done. He began the most historic accomplishment of his life—he would save the priceless treasures and art of Monte Cassino from inevitable destruction.

This personal campaign of his was hit with problem after problem.

First, he had to accomplish this solitary mission during his down time, off-duty, when he wasn't in combat and when his time—for the time being—was his own. But he was young and energetic and dedicated to his self-assigned mission, and he had an understanding Commandant, so with the blessing of the brass, Max managed to overcome this first obstacle.

His wife was not as understanding as his Commanding Officer. Wives rarely are. She and their family were back in Berlin, where things were degenerating—which meant bombs were falling near her and hers—so she wanted Max to return home whenever he could to attend to family matters, matters which fell under the title of "Get us out of here, get us out into the country, out where the bombs don't fall." Her desires were certainly understandable, and made Max's choices difficult. He wrestled with the problem and with great difficulty decided that irreplaceable, centuries old art would at times have to take precedence over personal issues. So he launched full-throttle into his campaign to save the treasures.

History does not report how the next few evenings at home with the family went for the good doctor.

Another obstacle: During his first meeting with Abbot Diamare, the old man had shown no interest in handing over Saint Benedict's treasures to this young German officer. The Abbot felt that the treasures would remain secure forever in the Monastery, to be watched over and protected by God and by man, mostly by God. The Abbot also was aware that the Germans had established a reputation not for saving great works of art, but for looting them. If he gave over the riches to this young officer, who could tell if they would wind up safe in the Vatican or in the trunk of some Nazi squad car, heading to Berlin.

Then there was the problem of the relics. The monks had bone chips from both Saint Benedict and his sister Scholastica.

Relics don't travel well. The Abbot would hate to see them damaged, or worse, hidden away in some war criminal's wine cellar after the war.

The Abbot's fears were warranted. Dr. Max was assigned to what was titled the Hermann Goering Division, and good old Hermann always seemed to have a birthday coming up. Goering, the Big Bird of the Luftwaffe, was second only to Hitler in the Reich, and all the boot-licking, ass-kissing young Nazis knew what Herm's favorite birthday present would be—a couple nice chunks of looted art. The H.G. Division was crawling with officers who would like nothing more than to impress their leader with some priceless and timeless knickknacks.

Dr. Max had no intention of allowing any of the Abbey's artwork to be sent back to the Fatherland. His plan called for every last piece to be crated, labeled, inventoried, and shipped directly to the Vatican, to be stored there until it could be safely returned to Monte Cassino after the war.

This led to another obstacle. Max would need trucks, plenty of them, along with shipping crates and storage supplies.

***

Mack: It's true. Whenever you've got a move coming up, it's hitting all the local stores begging for boxes. What a pain in the ass that is.

Scooter: And if you don't have access to a truck—have you seen the rental prices on those things? Especially with the drop-off rates.

Mack: You mean to tell me, with all your liquor places, you don't have a truck or two you can use?

Scooter: Sure, but that's me. I'm talking about the average guy, the guy without access. Of course, then too you have to talk a couple of your friends into helping you move. You can tell they don't want to do it, but you call in a few favors.

Mack: You've got to give this Dr. Max credit. It's hard for the average Joe.

***

Dr. Max *was* that average Joe—a Joe without access to any of the materials or equipment he would need for such a grand project—so off he went to the motor pool to snag some trucks and drivers. There the motor pool OIC heard him out, nodded his approval, but also dropped a few hints that some of the stuff—just a piece or two, you understand—would look awful nice up on Hermann Goering's mantle piece.

"Nothing doing," Max told him.

"Just kidding," was the motor pool chief's reply, but Max could tell he wasn't.

***

Scooter: Remember Ernie Bilko? He was a motor pool NCOIC, wasn't he?

Mack: Yeah, he was. Great show. Dr. Max should've thanked his Maltese Cross that Sergeant Ernie wasn't involved. He never would've seen a single stick of the stuff again.

Scooter: I don't know. Bilko always had great schemes, but they never seemed to work out for him. He was always left with nothing by the end of the show.

Mack: True. Fate and his own underlying humanity would always conspire against him. The best episode ever was when he went on the $64,000 Question. He's in the booth with his head bandaged up to cover the microphone receiver in his ear...

***

In securing the equipment necessary for the mission from the motor pool, Dr. Max inadvertently alerted his higher-level Chain of Command, and before he knew what had happened, a Lieutenant Colonel, a certain Julius Schlegel, had been put in charge of the operation. The two officers didn't like each other, each not trusting the other, and Julie Schlegel wound up getting the glory and eventually even received credit for the original idea.

But Dr. Max didn't mind that, he just wanted the job done—Julie out-ranked him, and Julie had the wherewithal to get things moving.

Light Colonel Julius Schlegel was a cultured Austrian, from Vienna—in his late forties, always smiling, joking, a great storyteller, the life of any party. He was also a Nazi, but we all have our faults.

Perhaps most important, he had owned his own transport business before the war, so he had the know-how needed for this project

Yes, Max had to admit, Julie would wind up doing a nice job.

One last obstacle for Max was his very limited command of Italian. Yet somehow, through gesture and facial expression and off-the-cuff pig Italian, he finally managed to convince the Abbot that the stuff would be much safer at the Vatican, and finally after much arguing and soul searching, the Abbot agreed.

Max also knew that the Abbot himself would be in danger when the front passed over, so he offered to haul the head monk to the Vatican for safekeeping along with the treasures. The Abbot was grateful, he appreciated Max's concern for his safety, but he refused to leave his Monastery.

All this happened months before the actual battle for Monte Cassino, and so at this point neither priest nor doctor ever thought the Monastery itself would be bombed. That was unthinkable. But the Germans had cozied up to within 300 meters of the sacred hilltop, so Max reminded the monk that bombs don't always drop where bombs are supposed to. "If you stay here, you might be killed, accidentally or not."

Like any other seventy-nine year old Italian *gum-bah* who had been running the show for thirty-four years, the Abbot just waved his hand in the air and said, "Mah, so I take a chance."

***

The old Abbot gathered his monks around him in the holiest spot in this holy place—the crypt of Saint Benedict—and with Saint Benedict's bones witness to his words, the Abbot in essence told his men: "Remember how you came to this holy place seeking an escape from the violent, messy world? To leave it behind for a life of heavenly predicable inner peace and piety? Well, forget all that. Some of you gotta hit the bricks." In Italian, it sounded better.

Soon the Monastery was filled with the noise and motion of manual labor—a "This Old House" episode without the construction. The Bob Villa of the show was Lieutenant Colonel Julius S. himself. His background in construction and transportation was perfectly suited for the project. Whether it had been he or Dr. Max who had been the original spearhead of the project was no longer important to either man. The bombs were getting closer, the Allies were advancing, war was thundering its destructive growl just over that hill to the south, so things must be moved, and moved quickly. Schlegel was the man who would do it. The lines of nationality had been blurred by war and—like Alec Guinness intent on building a beautiful bridge over the River Kwii, enemy project or not—Julius Schlegel was intent on getting the good stuff saved.

His workforce was made up of three diverse groups. One: the German soldiers in their gray-blue woolen uniforms, with jackets often hanging open at the chest but still with a certain regal military look, even if at the end of the sleeve was a hammer, nailing closed a crate of priceless artwork. Two: the dark-robed monks themselves, many of whom would eventually be leaving the monastery for Rome along with the nonhuman cargo. Three: in rags, the local Italians, willing to do anything, to go anywhere, simply to survive.

The three groups hauled the various crates out of the building and loaded them onto the waiting trucks that were lined up outside the brass doors, each with its motor running and the big "Hermann Goering Division" logo affixed to its door.

It was October, 1943, and the war was on its way. Schlegel got lumber, crates, nails and screws from an abandoned soda factory (most locals weren't buying soda these days) and he even managed to get a few skilled German carpenters assigned to the project.

Over a thousand peasants had sought shelter in the Abbey, but this mass of humanity did not provide much of a workforce. Most were women and children, many were sick, all were starving. Most of the able-bodied men had already been rounded up by the Germans and sent to Germany as slave laborers.

***

The haul....

The Monastery had housed one of the most extensive collections of art and culture in Europe.

Frescoes, paintings, miniatures, *objets d'art* both religious and secular. Thirty crates of archeological finds from nearby Pompeii. Ancient scrolls, mosaics, and Renaissance portraits. Goyas. Grecos. Parchments, relics, and coins.

The Monastery's library held over seventy thousand priceless documents to be transported. Over forty thousand manuscripts of guys like Cicero, Horace, Ovid and Virgil, works which centuries of pious monks had meticulously hand-lettered.

One monk, three centuries earlier, had been told one of his sins would be absolved for each letter he transcribed. When he completed the document, he proudly wrote that the letters had exceeded his previous sins by one. Imagine what this guy's nights on the town must have been like before he found God.

The haul also included creations by the great Italian masters, statues inlayed with gold and studded with jewels, varied ancient artifacts, original manuscripts by the English poets Keats and Shelley (which had been brought to the Abbey for safekeeping from the Keats-Shelley house in Rome) and, most important of all to the monks—relics of their name-sake Saint. And his sister.

Three hundred and eighty-seven cases of sacred magic.

Almost as an afterthought, the Germans offered to also ship out the monks and some civilians. To a man the monks wished that they could remain with their spiritual leader in their spiritual and material home—the Monastery—but obedience was one of the vows that they had taken when they had joined the order, obedience along with chastity and poverty—and so they would follow the orders that the Abbot had given them.

About eighty monks, thirty nuns, as well as a few orphans and students—all unsure of their destination—hopped on board the trucks.

Much had to be left behind: a large wooden sculpture of the Blessed Virgin, many books, Niko the Monastery's pet raven, one hundred fifty or so refugees, and of course the Abbot and those monks who had been chosen to stay put.

***

The monks had counted and labeled and recorded each item, determined that they would someday be returned to their rightful place and not end up as a Nazi tietack or cufflink.

With more and more American aircraft beginning to scream by overhead, the work continued. Finally, over one hundred Blitz brand name trucks, each loaded with civilization and *homo sapiens*, headed down the mountain. The funicular running down had been destroyed by aircraft months before and was unavailable. (The only reason I mention this fact is that I enjoy using the word "funicular.")

On the journey, not a single truck was destroyed by mountain accident or by enemy fire. A convoy of one hundred trucks—each clearly labeled "Hermann Goering Division"—had somehow survived the flight unscathed. The power of Saint Benedict perhaps? The sleepiness of some American artillery observer or fighter pilot?

***

Mack: (Singing, trying for the nasal tones of Willy Nelson): All the *federales* say, we could have had him any day, we only let him get away, out of kindness, I suppose.

***

Julie and Dr. Max had pulled off the unimaginable. Stupidity and destruction had been bested by civilization and skill. That almost never happens.

***

The Abbot had more right hand men than he had right hands, and one named Leccisotti had wished to remain in his beloved Monastery with his beloved leader, but the Abbot had ordered him to ride in the trucks along with the treasures and the monks. His mission would be twofold: Keep a close eye on the loot, and try to play some politics to keep the Monastery safe from destruction by either side.

In Rome Leccisotti would be running with the big dogs. Pope Pius XII could play the political game as well as anyone, and has often been criticized for buddy-ing up a bit too closely to Hitler and not doing enough to halt, or at least slow down, the Holocaust. When the Axis chances were looking pretty good, Pius had signed deals with Hitler and Mussolini. But now he could see that these two would wind up either gone nuts in a bunker or hanging from his heals in the town square, so the Pontiff's biggest fear these days was of the atheistic Communism of Joe Stalin.

Still, it was the Germans occupying his city, and the city around his city, and the local comedians' favorite line had become, "The Pope these days, he's closer to Himmler than to *himmel* (heaven.)" It was wartime; humor was at a premium.

Mussolini, for all of his brown-shirted buffoonish bluster, had at least not allowed Hitler to haul the Jews out of Italy, or from occupied France, off to the gas chambers. Now that Mussolini had been reduced to no more than a Jack Oakie imitation in a Charlie Chaplin movie, Hitler sent his Storm Troopers out onto the streets of Italy to round up the Jews for extermination. America begged the Pontiff to speak out against this atrocity, but he was too scared; instead he fell back on that old song of an excuse: "Well, we can't really be sure."

Hitler had probably told Pius that the Jews were being sent to a nice little farm upstate where boys and girls would love them and treat them nice and let them play with puppies.

***

This Leccisotti was a scholar, a man of the cloth, not a politician, but he managed to get an audience with Cardinal Maglione, the papal Secretary of State, and there made his case for keeping the Monastery from any harm. Mags told him that he would forward the message to the Pope. In the meantime—Don't call us, we'll call you.

Hard to believe, but a few days later they did. Leccisotti was told that the Pope's man wanted to see him. Leccisotti walked through the sad and starving streets of Rome and arrived at the Vatican. There he was told that the Pope would write a message asking the Germans not to occupy the Monastery of Saint Benedict in Monte Cassino. The Germans would oblige.

The Pope also promised to send a message to the Allies, asking them to please keep this holy place neutral and unharmed, since that's what the Germans were doing.

A hell of a lot of good *that* message did.

***

Dr. Max continued to keep an eye on the treasures, making sure none of them were shipped to Goering's private ill-gotten stash. A few times he had to challenge and warn some superior officers who appeared to be more interested in brown-nosing than in protecting civilization.

Would anybody be surprised that all this activity would finally land Max in some deep shit with his superior officers? In December the Doctor was called on the carper by the Chief Medical Officer of the Hermann Goering Division. Dr. Max's got his ass soundly chewed for, among other things, sticking his big nose where it did not belong (it apparently belonged buried somewhere deep in Goering's coccyx), for dereliction of duty, and, worst of all, for acting like a civilized and concerned human being. Uncalled for wartime conduct.

Max of course had no excuse, even though his outfit had given him permission to take on the mission, and he had always acted on his off-duty time, and only after making sure all of his medical duties were taken care of, with proper support in place.

Dr. Max tried to explain that he had acted for the good of European Civilization.

The Chief Medical Officer thundered back at him that, if he wanted to help civilization, he always could do it from the Russian Front. This was the response and threat used ubiquitously throughout German-controlled Europe during those years:

"Sir, my breakfast biscuits are lice-infested."

"Oh, perhaps you'd like to eat those biscuits on the Russian Front."

"Sir, excuse me, sir, you're standing on my foot."

"Oh, perhaps you would like me to stand on your foot on the Russian Front."

"Sir, I have dysentery, may I report to sick bay?"

"Certainly you may, but only if that aforementioned sick bay is on the Russians Front."

"Sir, I hate to say it—the war is lost."

"Oh, and perhaps you'd like to inform us all that the war was lost on the Russian Front?!"

Well, it *was*, but nobody was going to come right out and say it, and back in Berlin, his stooges were all telling Hitler how well things were going, war-wise. That was right after they got done telling him that he had been a very successful wallpaper-hanger in Austria between wars—that people in Vienna were still talking about how swell their living room looked since they had brought in Adolph. He matched patterns like no one else. His artwork with a broad brush of paper glue was legendary.

At the termination of his ass-chewing, Dr. Max was shipped out of southern Italy. He was sent to a Luftwaffe command in Bologna, up north. He was out of the civilization-saving game, but his mission had been accomplished.

And at least he had not been told: "Head north, Cap'm, then make yourself a quick and sharp right-hand turn and keep walking until you hear the term, *Smirnoff*."

***

On January 12, 1944, Hermann Goering had his fifty-first birthday party. The Reich-Marshal was known as "The Iron Man" when he was in the room, and "The Fat One" when he wasn't—either way, the man was one large looter, one of the largest in history.

This birthday celebration was especially lavish, since everyone in attendance and involved in the planning realized that there wouldn't be too many more of these celebratory occasions for the Reich.

The birthday boy found himself surrounded by fine cuisine, excellent wines and champagnes, waiters gussied-up in white uniforms, guests with phony and hopeless smiles, rare books stolen from the private libraries of exterminated Jews, and enough loot to bring a smile to the face of any Nazi war criminal. He busied himself unwrapping boxes of fine cigars and gold bars and—just what he had asked for—a bust of Hitler.

***

Mack: I would've been happy with just the gold bars and cigars.
Scooter: Hitler *was* a bust.

***

But a few things were absent from the party.

Colonel Julie was said to be not in attendance. Although, with Light Colonel Schlegel, you could never really tell. He had posed for pictures of his H.G. Division delivering the riches of Saint Benedict to the Vatican at the Castel Sant' Angelo, only to later insist he had not been there at all.

Nor was Max in attendance at the party. Captain-Doctor Max, who had managed to sneak home to see his family in Tecklenburg, was still worried about all that Russian Front stuff, but did not share his concerns with the little lady.

And also missing…

Some of the loot. The monks had kept careful records of the crates that had left their Monastery heading for the Vatican. Some of the treasures were those from the Naples collection. Some had been diverted to Spoleto, but the German Command insisted they had then all been taken to Rome for safekeeping.

When the trucks had arrived in Rome, fifteen crates were missing, unaccounted for. Oh well, a few of the trucks had been delayed by machinegun fire, the monks were told, but the monks hadn't heard any shooting. "Delayed by machinegun fire" was obviously an early rendition of the phrase "Fell off a truck."

Herr Goering had officially received no gift at all from his eponymous Division. But he had a few secret passages in Karin Hall, his mansion. A bit later in the year, he brought his pal Albert Speer down there. "Lookit all this stuff, would you" he told Speer, "Lookit these paintings. Here, here, smell this French perfume, isn't that incredible? Oh, oh, taste this wine…can you believe it?...okay, okay, that's enough, leave a little for somebody else. All this stuff, and it's all stolen from the mules of civilization, the poor, dumb, schmucks who are too ignorant to deserve it and too weak to hold onto it. Oh, oh, and best thing...lookit all these art treasures I got from Italy, from Naples...oh, oh, and..."

***

Yet, for the most part, the treasures of Monte Cassino had been saved from the ravages of war.

And now Petoola and the Allied Commanders were finishing up licking their wounds from the *Rapido* blood bath. The Monastery had been a convenient excuse for their failure to take the Valley. Now that they had reduced the ancient place to rubble, it was time for a renewed attack. This one could not fail.

***

"…Two…"

Chapter Nine:
After the Demolition

"...in his reckless way
Mocking the lazy brotherhood, deplores
The illuminated manuscripts, that lay
Torn and neglected on the dusty floors"

-from "Monte Cassino" by Henry Wadsworth Longfellow 1875

***

Any military advantage that was to be gained by the demolition of the Monastery would be based on two suppositions: 1. the German position would be weakened; 2. the bombing would immediately be followed by a quick, decisive attack.

The idea: The Germans would no longer have a safe haven from which to observe the enemy and from which to zero in their artillery fire. In addition, the Germans would be shattered, weakened, and disoriented by the unexpected bombing and thus be ill-prepared for a quick, frontal ground assault.

And monkeys have wings.

As everyone knows by now, the Germans weren't even occupying the place. They were *close* to the Monastery, closer than the three hundred meters they had promised and that they were telling the world, but they were not actually *in* the place. They had no reason to be. They had perfectly good observation posts and strongholds set up at various distances along the Cassino Mastiff, that snake-deadly ridge running above the *Liri* Valley. Their positions did not have romantic or historic names, like *The Monastery at Monte Cassino.* They simply had military designations like Point (or Hill) 593, Point 569, Point 503, Point 444, Point 445, Point 236. Boring stuff. A few would be assigned labels with a bit more pizzazz—Hangman's Point, Phantom Ridge, the Albaneta Farm, but the point is, these were the positions that should have been hit by the Flying Fortresses and by the light bombers.

True, it would not have looked as good on the war maps, would not have provided as much dramatic power for the Movietone News, but strategically, these little outposts were the links in the chain of the German positioning. "Hit him where he lives," American football coaches have been telling their linemen since the days of Red Grange (meaning, "Hit him in the balls"), but the advice was never given to the war planners of Monte Cassino, and, if given, not heeded.

As for the second advantage, the "softening up" of the Gustav Line for a full frontal attack (long before that term had acquired Playboy Magazine connotations), the window for such an attack would be a narrow one at best.

Before a single bomber had ever taken off from the Foggia runways, the Allied commanders knew that they had no troops in position for a quick follow-up. Since American and British troops were tired, dazed, and mostly dead from the first little move across the *Rapido* and the Valley, it was decided that troops from India and New Zealand would be the tigers (or the sacrificial lambs) this time up the Massif.

Not even Jeeps could be used to get supplies, much less men, into position to attack the Germans; remember, those paths were often not more than eighteen inches wide. The men had to stumble up the inclines in darkness, loaded down and scared. So many mules had already been slaughtered that the men often had to carry double and triple packs.

The Indian troops who were assigned the task of launching the post-demolition attack had been told that the Americans had secured the critical Point 593, but in truth the position was still held by the Germans. The nearby Americans were in such terrible shape that they had to be taken back down the hills on stretchers. And those were the lucky ones. Many of the other Americans were now simply khaki-wearing cadavers—long dead and rotting under the Italian sun. An Indian foot soldier came upon a couple of the poor stiffs and tried to look on the bright side: "Thank God their mothers couldn't see the sadness and indignity of it all." Which basically summed up the entire campaign.

The second attack on the Monastery was given the code name "Operation Avenger," but I'm not sure that one can avenge one's own stupidity.

***

This second Allied attack was being coordinated by the New Zealander with the Jewish name, General Bernie Freyberg, a barrel-chested six-footer directly below Petoola in the Allied Chain of Command. Freyberg called up the Indian commander, Dimoline, and told him that the B-17's were about to bomb the crap out of the Monastery. "Your boys all good and ready, are they?"

"No."

The Indian told Freyberg that the demolition of the Monastery would have to be put off. His troops up on the Massif were not ready to launch an attack from that strategic stepping stone, Hill (Point) 593; first they would have to *capture* strategic stepping stone Hill (Point) 593. An air attack now would be pointless and senseless.

"Sorry, mate, time to go."

Freyberg went on to explain to the Indian that the bombers would hit late morning, maybe around noon. Dimoline again objected. That meant that even if his troop were ready to attack, the attack would have to be made in broad, killing daylight. "Let's put things off a while." I remind you that none of these " " are historic quotes, but merely shallow recreations. What Dimoline probably *really* said was, "For Christ sake, let's put things off a while," then adding a derogatory appellation.

And in essence the response was: "Sorry, mate, photo op. Let's go."

Yes, Freyberg knew beforehand that the destruction of the Monastery would serve no military purpose, but, like Petoola, he was a General with a reputation and maybe even a career on the line. He had been brought in to get things moving and, by God, that is what he was going to do. Nothing would be placed on hold as long as he was running the show. If the destruction of the Monastery was not going to help, well then, the battle would have to be won solely by the best and bravest soldiers in the world—his New Zealanders, along with those jolly, baldheaded fellows from India. With the big grins and the big knives.

***

In one respect, Freyberg was absolutely correct. If one needed an oily, deadly, horrible job to be done on the battlefield, his were the troops to do it, or to die trying. Of course, it was a foregone conclusion that they *would* die trying, but these boys would get the job done all right.

When those all around you are losing their heads—from mortar fire or artillery—you can't do better than to keep your head among the helmets of the Kiwis and the Gurkhas.

The New Zealanders were a close-knit crew of buddies, many of whom had known each other since childhood, had grown up together, joined up together, and if need be, would die together.

One often overlooked element of warfare is the fact that young men in the field find themselves fighting and dying not for their country, not for their God, certainly not for their officers, but rather for their fellow foot soldiers. Get a group who has been together and known each other for awhile, maybe for a lifetime, and you'll have a more efficient and selfless fighting man—one who certainly looks out for himself, but also takes care of the man standing there next to him, peeking out from the dark shadow of his low-slung helmet.

***

Scooter: How'd that work for us? I didn't know you from Lon Chaney, and I didn't want to.
Mack: That's why I never did anything to save *your* fucken life—all the time for me over there it was *my* fucken life I was planning to come home with. Intact.
Scooter: Good for you.

***

The Gurkhas and other fighting men of the Indian subcontinent might not have grown up together, but they *had* all grown up in a culture which showed them what bravery and viciousness looked like when stirred together. It looked a lot like they did: dark-skinned, scowling killers with shaved heads and sharpened knives. Take away a Gurkha's rifle (as if you could), then take away his knife (as if you could), and he would kill you with his stare.

***

Mack: They also make fine cigars.

***

These men, these New Zealanders and these Gurkhas, were the ones assigned the second assault on Monte Cassino: the Z's to attack from below, Gurkhas to battle their way across that promontory with the prophetic name of Snake's Head Ridge.

Both groups would die there.

***

Ironically, the bombing of the Abbey had created a perfect defensive venue for the Germans. Now they no longer had to observe the three hundred meter holy zone; all holiness had been done away with; in military terminology: "All pertinent materials had been committed to special destruction activity." Only the bottom few feet of the massive walls of the Abbey were still standing, surrounded by acres of concrete and granite rubble.

A perfect place to defend, to hide, to kill anyone advancing upon it. Simply rest your gun muzzle on a rock and wait. The mule paths along the top of Snake's Head Ridge were so narrow that at many points soldiers had to advance one-by-one. Like in a shooting gallery.

Perfect. Perfect. Let the swine come.

***

The Punjabi (Indian) men of the Sussex Division, advancing along Snake's Head Ridge, trying to get themselves ready for a post-bombing attack, had been surprised to look up and see the huge fleet of Flying Fortresses overhead. At first they though the planes might be German. They watched the destruction of the Monastery in awe and amazement. Remember: the press had been told about the imminent bombing of the Monastery, the monks had been told, the civilian and military big-wigs had been told ("Bring a lunch, enjoy yourself"), but nobody had bothered to tell the guys who were supposed to follow-up the bombing with an attack.

Freyberg finally got word to the Battalion that the Monastery was being destroyed, and Point 593 was in friendly hands, so let's get a move on.

"No, it's not. No, we won't."

When they *did* begin to move forward across the top of Snake's Head Ridge, in that "Ducks in a Shooting Gallery" single file, the troops met the well-positioned Germans, who had no problem in simply picking them off. Anyone even remotely connected to the British Empire has an inbred talent for understatement, so the Indian commander stated his men's position to be "uncomfortable."

Uncomfortable. Uncomfortable is when you're in your recliner with the TV on and a beer in your hand and a loose spring starts jabbing you a bit in your ass. Not this.

That night, as they moved across the ridge, the troops were not even sure they were on the right path. Still, they preferred the darkness to sunlight, or to those blinding flashes of German artillery—shelling that killed them as it illuminated their position.

These brave men of the Sussex up on Snake's Head Ridge had hoped that the fighter-bombers of the Allies would blanket-cover Point 593 with the bombs, thus making their advance at least a bit tenable, but by now they were too close to that point and any bombing would have killed as many of them as Germans.

Then they ran out of hand grenades, and ran low on ammunition; they had to wait for another convoy of mules to resupply them. If you think a mule moves slowly under normal conditions, try being defenseless and waiting for them to get there with your only hope of survival. These beasts take their own sweet time.

The mules finally did arrive, the men stocked up on grenades, some of them managed to advance as far as the 593, the Germans counterattacked, the Sussex men ran out of grenades again, the mules had gone back home, the Germans set off green flares to better spot and kill, the Sussex men knew that a green flare from their own side was a signal to retreat, it was getting light out, so...*Run away! Run away!*

Back down the ridge a ways, breathing so heavy that their faces and eyes ached, the men of Sussex looked around, counting their mates. Half were no longer there; and the few survivors knew they would never see these childhood chums again.

***

Freyberg found himself in the same position Petoola had been in after the attempted crossing of the *Rapido*. His men had been slaughtered; his reputation had a suffered a skinned knee. He reacted in the exact same way Petoola had. He ordered another attack, this one in the daylight, this one even more suicidal for his men than the first.

***

Mack: What do they teach these fuggers in Command School? Can't there be *one* lecture, at least, entitled, "When it comes down to your men or your rep, save your men, for Christ sake, preserve your fucken men."
Scooter: Lousy name for a lecture. How would that look in the Syllabus of Studies?

***

Freyberg insisted that this next attack would prove successful because it would be launched on a much larger scale, with many more men advancing up the hill. Going up, but not coming back down.

***

Mack: Yeah, still walking single file.

***

Another pressure to get things done quickly: the Allied landing at Anzio was not going well. The forces on the beach were in danger of being driven back into the sea by the German counterattack. If the Germans succeeded here, it would be a far worse defeat than the evacuation at Dunkirk. There, British citizens had taken rowboats and canoes and pleasure crafts across the English Channel to help rescue their soldiers. There would be no English rowboats sailing down around Gibraltar into the Mediterranean to save their blokes this time.

The Kiwi/Gurkha attack at Monte Cassino had been planned and ordered not only to secure the Valley, but to force the Germans to pull a large portion of their forces from Anzio so that Hitler's precious Gustav Line could be protected.

So Freyberg, with Petoola bugging him about Anzio, had ordered this follow-up attack; he coordinated the high ground attack with a Kiwi attack down in the *Rapido* Valley. "The old one-two. These Krauts won't know what hit them."

Yeah, right.

***

Down by the *Rapido*, more flooding, more rain, more sweat, had turned things even more mucky and murky.

Per Freyberg's order, the Kiwis moved forward through this soggy mess. Even when they were on relatively dry ground, they encountered mines and barbed wire. The Germans were hitting them with ear-splitting, flesh-burning mortar fire. A Kiwi Captain with the incongruously whimsical name of Wikiriwhi—who was serving there along with two of his brothers, the Wikiriwhi boys—ordered a charge. Like the selfless, friends-and-family surrounded men that they were, the first few Kiwis threw their bodies on the strings of barbed wire so that their mates could advance by running across their backs.

Then they fought the Germans hand-to-hand, with bayonets, fists, kicks and curses. There was no time to look skyward with the hopes of seeing air cover, but if there had been time for that, all the brave Zealanders would have seen was that Snake's Head against the sky, where the Gurkhas were faring no better than they were.

***

The Indians were still trying to secure and hold onto Hill 593, the "Monte Calvario" of prewar times. Some of the bombs intended for the Monastery had "softened up" this area all right, but unfortunately had fallen on and thus "softened up" the *Indian* troops, not the Germans. Sometimes two wrongs don't make a right, they just lead to another wrong.

More than half of the men of a single company—thirty-two men and two of the three officers—had been killed trying to stumble forward in the dark, over loose rock and deep gullies, directly into withering German machinegun fire.

Freyberg was still desperately hoping to salvage his resume. He had been the one to strongly advocate the destruction of the Monastery. He had been the one to promise that soon after the air strike, the area would fall, leading to clear sailing up to Rome. Now, a couple of hours and a couple of deadly attacks later, his men were in no better position than they had been before the mass bombing.

Since nothing has changed since the first aborted attack that he had ordered, he had naturally ordered that second attack, this time trying to capture *both* Hill 593 and the Monastery itself. History does not record what could have given him the dimwitted idea that things would work out fine this time up the hill. The paths were still treacherous, the supplies were still low, the resupply routes were still long, arduous, and nearly impassible. The Germans were still willing to shoot either fish in a barrel, ducks in a pond, or Gurkhas stumbling single-file up the hill, whatever came their way.

One other thing had remained unchanged—the Gurkhas still held their nearly superhuman, unbelievable courage. And, unlike many of Petoola's troops, the Kiwi boys still held their commander in high regard. There would be no postwar investigation into Freyberg's stupidity.

Only sixty percent of the Royal Sussex had survived their previous trip up the hill, but up the hill again they went. The Gurkhas managed to belly-crawl along the jagged rocks until they were no more than four hundred yards from the ruins of the famous Abbey. From there, through the smoke, they could make out a high patch of bramble bush, blowing in the breeze between them and their target. With war whoops worthy of their aboriginal ancestry, they ran toward those bushes—once there they could use the high growth for some shelter from the German guns.

It was one more black bead of a mistake in an entire rosary of mistakes. The Germans had laced those bushes with tripwires attached to antipersonnel land mines. Gurkhas leggings were entwining with two, three, and four wires as the S-mines took apart their legs and their bodies. In less than a quarter of an hour, two-thirds of the Gurkhas had been killed. When the mines and booby traps had all been exploded, more Gurkhas tried to advance into and then through the thicket, stepping over and upon the bodies of their comrades. They ran directly into Germans machinegun fire. Another group of Gurkhas who had tried a slightly different route moved into a box canyon of bullets coming from three sides at once. They tried frantically to dig some protective covering from the rocky surface of the mountainside. Protection could not be dug.

***

Both Hemingway and the Bible tell us that the sun also rises, and the next day it rose on the shambles of the Allied attack. When Freyberg had doubled the number of men to be used in the last attack, all he accomplished was a doubling of the deaths of his men. Five hundred and thirty Indian soldiers had lost their lives. It was obvious to everyone that the destruction of the Monastery had changed nothing. Frontal assault was a death trap and nothing more.

So General Freyberg's keen military mind came up with a new plan: he now suggested *another* attack, just like the others.

What is that definition of insanity? Something about doing the same thing over and over again expecting different results? If there were anything to laugh about, Freyberg's suggestion would have been laughed out of the ballpark. As it were, he was gently talked out of the plan.

The Americans and the British had been destroyed in the first series of attacks. New Zealanders and Indians had been decimated in this second series.

What was left to do then, what was left to try? Think of a new strategy maybe? Map out a new route up to Rome? Concentrate men and materials on the upcoming Normandy invasion instead? Admit finally that this half-assed, senseless slaughter of good men in Italy had to stop now?

Well, could be any of that. Or else we could just look around for something else to bomb the hell out of.

***

Chapter Ten:
Destruction of a Town

"Below, the darkening town grew desolate."

-from "Monte Cassino" by Henry Wadsworth Longfellow 1875

***

The obliteration of the Monastery had gone so well—destroying hundreds of innocent lives and centuries of civilization without securing even a single military benefit—and had been so dog-gone photogenic—that it is little wonder the boys in charge next decided to obliterate the town of Cassino itself.

Without the Monastery in its history, the town of Cassino would have been just another anonymous little farming community of southern Italy, no more notable than surrounding communities like Cervaro, Frosinone and Latina, destined to live out its existence in relative obscurity and peace.

The town was founded by an ancient group of Italian people called the Volsci, and then invaded and controlled by somebody called the Samnites, and then of course by the Romans, who established a colony there in 312 B.C.

For a brief time in modern history, the town was known as San Germano, but the name soon reverted back to the original Cassino.

The region is called Ciociaria, and its topology and climate have been compared to those of northern California, with gentle hills, nourishing rivers, and mild seasons. These hills can trap the fog in the winter, at times turning the weather chilly and foreboding, but rarely brutal. Summers can be hot and humid, but never intimidating.

The town lies comfortably snuggled against the granite and limestone walls of the mountains, some eighty miles south of Rome. The populace in 1943 consisted mostly of farmers and peasants, along with the requisite craftsmen and merchants. Other than grapes, the main crop was the sap and the fruit of the small, twisted olive trees—trees that were planted and cultivated in the meadows in lines as straight as a phalanx of Roman soldiers.

The *Liri* Valley was lush and well irrigated by the waters of the *Rapido* and *Garigliano* rivers. The snowcapped Abruzzi Mountains offer a postcard backdrop to the Valley, while Cassino itself usually does not suffer snowy winters. The winter of 1943-1944 was an aberration, an aberration of the worst sort—an aberration which came at the worse time.

Other than Saint Benedict and his sister, the most famous visitors to the town throughout its history include King Totila, who visited in 543, and Saint Thomas Aquinas, who was a student of the Benedictines beginning in 1225. Because of the prestige of the Benedictines, the town became the scene of papal politics from time to time, such as when Pope Leo IX visited to arrange some back room deals there in 1057.

At the beginning of the hostilities of the Second World War, the town's population hovered around 25,000.

But for the most part, this Latium town remained a quiet, peaceful farming village. The people, as well as the town itself, simply minded their own business and didn't mind at all if history quietly passed them by.

The town officially covered a respectable one hundred sixty acres, but much of that was undeveloped or agricultural land. In the village area itself, no fewer than four churches provided spiritual guidance and support for the population. And for those who chose to reject that guidance and support, the town had its own small courthouse and prison. There were schools and shops and even two luxurious hotels.

A nearby hot springs was used for treating the body and soul; the ruins of temples and an amphitheater gave adults a bit of history to talk about and gave the kids some neat places to play.

In the vineyards it seemed nearly every farmer had his own special secret method for making wine. Year after year, the hottest political issue centered around the making of pesto sauce—do you grind or mash your garlic and *pignoli* nuts?

A few farmers tried their hand at tobacco growing and cigar making, attempting to emulate the success of the Garibaldi brand (which is still a popular smoke for Italians, especially since Clint Eastwood looked so tough when clutching one of those stogies in his mouth in all of those Sergio Leone spaghetti westerns).

Each weekend, the farmers of the Valley would bring their produce into the town, and the day would be spent buying, selling, bartering, borrowing, lending, and gossiping. The square would be filled not only with people, but with cows, sheep, and mules. The mules were as serene and naïve as the people—neither had any idea of what was about to hit them.

On special holy days, the statue of the Madonna would be carried through the streets, with long strips of brightly colored ribbons streaming from her shoulders, as the townspeople would put on their special costumes and sing and dance in the square. On those special days, abetted by warm wine and warmer friendship, the pasta sauce would take on a special mysterious taste, as the mozzarella and ricotta would grow smoother and tastier.

A few noble families erected and kept huge, sumptuous villas just outside of the village. The most distinguished nobleman would be referred to as "Our Prince," since Italy had been a unified country for only eighty years, and many occupants still thought of this young country in terms of separate principalities and kingdoms.

All in all, the town was borderline prosperous, satisfied, content, and assured that all things had remained the same for a thousand years and would stay that way for a thousand more.

***

So really—why not bomb the hell out of the place?

Why not hit this little village with an intense storm of incendiary destruction the likes of which had never before been witnessed in all the history of the human race?

***

In March, 1944, roughly a month after American bombers had reduced the center of European civilization on the hill to a pile of hot rocks, spring was in the air and weather reports were predicting an unbroken string of summerlike days.

Perfect weather for another foolhardy infantry attack on the dug-in enemy. This attack would be conducted once again by the New Zealand troops and the troops of India. Most of the population of the town of Cassino had already fled; approximately three hundred German paratroopers had taken their place and were now occupying the town. Not a huge number, but enough of an obstacle to halt Allied military progress.

A rumble was heard from the south. The Kiwis looked skyward. The blue sky suddenly became a backdrop for more heavy duty aircraft than anyone had ever seen flying in one formation at one time.

The town was about to be escorted into history. In a few hours, it would no longer exist. The tiny, one square mile surface of the village area would be replaced by hot craters and open stone foundations that seemed to be screaming in pain up to the sky.

***

Scooter: A mile square, huh? Nothing much. That was the size of the town I grew up in.

Mack: I thought you rubes out there had so much land that the hick towns could spread out for miles. God's country.

Scooter: Well, yeah, it was God's country all right—it was only me and Him out there, and I got drafted. But, no, my town itself was small. Just a single neighborhood, really, everybody knows everybody. Good place to grow up.

Mack: Mine too.

Scooter: Brooklyn? What are you talking about? Brooklyn's got two million people. When you say "small," you must be talking about the mental capacity, not the population.

Mack: No, moron, I was speaking of Sheepshead Bay. A bumpkin such as yourself wouldn't realize that any large city is just a pack of small neighborhoods pressed together by necessity. Where I grew up, everybody knew everybody, all the mothers looked out for all the kids. Just like Cassino, the town, before we showed up there, just like out where you are, except we had paved streets to walk on, instead of miles and miles of cow shit. Or, what was it you had, cattle shit? Mountain goat shit? Some kind of shit, I know that for sure.

Scooter: I can't help imagining what those bombers could've done to Merchant—that was the name of mine. What the war could've done. My God.

Mack: You can't go thinking like that. Forget it.

Scooter: All these years later, I still get thoughts like that sometimes. I'll look out at a busy street, happy folks, hustling along, smiling at one another, maybe like those poor lambs in Italy were, before the war came along.

Mack: Us, them, it screwed us all up.

Scooter: It did.

Mack: With me, it made me scared, I'm always…can I tell you this?…I'm always…not for me, but for my kids mostly, my son mostly, I read the papers, I think, "What if?" What if? I get unreasonably scared for him. I'm always thinking…what if something was to happen? Then what? He's growing up now, Eddie, almost grown up, I still worry the hell out of him. It's the war, the war still remains with me. I don't bother to tell people, but it's there. All the time, sometimes. In stretches.

Scooter: Yeah it is.

Mack: It screwed us all up for good, didn't it, being there for that, for what we saw and even what we did. I'm not saying I would prefer I would have been left dead over there, face down in some pile of mule shit like a lot of our guys were, with no one even bothering to read my dog tags, figure out who the hell I am, or else get my leg blown off, or my cock or my arms gone. Both arms sometimes—I've seen guys like that, you have too. No, I was lucky. We were both of us lucky, the two of us, in the minority, but still, what I'm saying…here for instance, my kid's about ten years old, he's up on the roof of our building, they're playing punch ball, bunch of neighborhood ankle-biters playing punch ball up there, that's nothing, not that dangerous or anything, I did the same thing myself a hundred times as a kid, still though, I catch him up there, I panic, I'm so scared I'm trembling, I'm grabbing him by the arm, "What the hell you doing, don't you know you could get hurt up here? Supposing you fell off, then what?" He's looking at me like I'm crazy, he's scared. I drag him down to the apartment, I gave him the beating of his life. Lots of…lots of…hits. I'm crying, he's crying. We don't talk about it now, never did. I think he's maybe forgotten, at least forgotten the ferocity of it, the fear. I hope so. But what that was, that was the war hitting him, cutting up his little face like that, strap marks. It wasn't me doing that, it was the war. That's what I like to tell myself. You were always stronger than I was, Scoot, you got back, I bet, you managed to put it behind you. I couldn't do that.

Scooter: No, well, with me, it was I had to keep moving all the time. Couldn't ever just sit still. It was work, work, work, work, work, work, work. My wife couldn't slow me down. Like an engine, it blows out its governor, so it's just revving and revving, steaming, burning itself out, out of control. Gonna eventually smoke and steam and seize up. I never really saw my kids grow up. They grew up, I'm out tending to the business. The good part—I made a lot of money. The bad part—nobody cares about that. Me neither.

***

For hour after hour, the bombers flew over the town of Cassino, dropping their slim metal chambers of death. It was not the media event that the bombing of the Monastery had been, but it was twice as many bombs this time, a thousand tons of explosives, a *thousand tons*, dropped on an area not much bigger than the Monastery had been. A thousand tons. With that much bulk, it didn't even have to be bombs and incendiaries coming down. You drop a thousands tons of *anything* on a small village and it's going to come out crushed into nothing. You drop a thousand tons of feathers, of Hershey bars, of anything, on a little town like that, and the place is gone, it's gone.

Carpet bombing. Over five hundred and seventy-five bombers. For three and a half hours—Fortresses, Mitchells, Liberators. *Liberators*—that was their name. Two hundred fighters-bombers. The largest air force ever assembled in that part of the war. More bombs than could ever be counted, or imagined. It was as though all the frustrations of that winter were coming out, bubbling up to the surface. *Okay, if we can't win, we can still destroy, destroy.*

***

Mack: The funniest movie I ever saw? A little twenty minute one-reeler, Stan and Ollie again, Laurel and Hardy…

Scooter: What, them in the Alps again, moving a piano across the footbridge?

Mack: No, this is a different one.

Scooter: We talking about the same thing here? Cassino? Henry was telling us about the town, right?

Mack: I am too. Eventually. Listen. What I'm saying, this movie, almost no plot to it. It's just the two of them, Stan and Ollie, they're wrecking this guy's house, while he's out in the street wrecking their car, their Model T. It's the little guy with the big mustache, they were always fighting him. Who do I mean?

Scooter: Jimmy Finlayson.

Mack: Yeah, Jimmy Finlayson. So, the boys aren't quite done reducing his house to rubble, but he's all done doing their car, there's nothing left of it. So what does he do? He takes a stick, a bat, and just starts pounding the rubble. Just to have something to do. Just to keep himself busy. Well see, that's what the bombing raid on the town was—just all the frustration coming out. Hey, here's something we can do. It's: We can't manage to get those damn Nazi paratroopers out of our way so we can on get to Rome, but we sure as hell can keep pounding the village the poor dumb-ass Italians used to live in. Make sure nothing alive ever comes around *here* anymore.

***

Even the New Zealanders, who were stationed closer than anyone—a couple hundred yards away—kept waiting for the bombing to stop, hoping it would: *What's the point, the town is gone, gone. That's enough.*

At first the bombs dropped with pinpoint precision, but after a few explosions so much dust and smoke was kicked up that the bombardiers could no longer make out the target. But they kept dropping anyway. After not too long, the friendly Moroccans and the British and the fearful mules were all being hit and killed, hit and killed by what they call "friendly fire." The mission had long ago been accomplished, now the bloodbath was hitting the guys on *our* side, but the bombing still did not stop. Three and a half hours of it.

Go watch: YouTube.com/watch?v=G14UNe7cMOg, or Search there for: "A Soldiers Story, Part 1." The bombing of the town.

One entire squadron of bombers didn't even hit the *right* town. Instead of Cassino, they bombed the town of Venafro, almost twenty miles away, and killed the confused people over there. Pilot looking out the window: "That looks like it. You think?"

Answer: "Close enough. Let's give it a try."

Nearly one hundred and fifty civilians died or were wounded in the bombings. Countless Allied fighting men were killed. Far more friendly troops and peasants were killed than were Germans. Still, the bombers kept coming.

Even some of those fearless Gurkhas were going crazy by now, because of the madness from above. They left their hiding places and ran out into the fields to scream up at the bombers.

The bombers kept coming.

***

Mack: And Jimmy Finlayson kept pounding that rubble.

***

A group of German paratroopers were hunkering down in the town—directly under the carpet bombing—were huddled together in a cellar of one of the town's old buildings. The smoke and dust clogged the air in the room so much that they could not see their own hands. They pressed together into one small knot of terrified humanity. Razor chips from the stone foundation laced across their hands and faces. Each time the bombing would stop, they would say a few words to each other in the darkness. "Rudolph? Heimi? You still there, *freund*?" Each knew that nothing—no one—could survive a bombing like this one. But each time, Rudolph answered. Heimi was still there. And then, each time, after a few more minutes, the bombs would start exploding again. There was no end to it.

Some squads of Germans paratroopers were buried alive. They would hear a stretch of silence, then somehow dig their way up to the surface. Then more planes would arrive, with more bombs, and they would be buried alive a second time. It was a loop-reel movie of an Edgar Allan Poe story, buried alive, again and again and again.

The buried men had to keep their mouths wide open, or else their eardrums would get blown out. But this meant that with each breath they were taking, they were also sucking in the dust and dirt.

They were worse than mules now, they were rats.

***

Afterwards, an American Air Force officer declared the town to be officially "fumigated."

No rat could have survived the operation.

***

The Germans watching the onslaught from the surrounding hills agreed. They watched their countrymen being bombed to death for hours. The "Oh, those poor swine" sentiment was replaced by, "And I am so glad it's not me down there."

***

The peasants who had once taken refuge in the Monastery, and were now scattered about the area—living in caves if they were lucky, in fields with no shelter at all if they had to—looked down at what once had been their town.

A few months before, they had thought the war would pass them by like a quick-moving, gray, autumn rain cloud. The Americans would sweep north, throwing candy from the back of their trucks and their Jeeps, and then they would leave them be. The farm families would be allowed to go back to their homes and farms and fields, to take up their lives again.

Now the poor victims stooped on the hillsides and gazed down at the pillars of smoke. Nothing else was there.

***

Finally there was quiet, and the New Zealand troops entered the town. They were pleased that for once they could move forward meeting no resistance. They saw not a town, but a scene of Biblical destruction. Piles of rock could not even be recognized as a building. A few low pieces of wall had managed to remain upright here and there, but not a single roof was intact.

One thousand tons of shells had been dropped on an area the size of a neighborhood. And it showed. Huge bomb craters had destroyed the streets. The craters were filling with water and mud.

Acrid smoke filled the air. Dust covered everything.

On the outskirts of the town, the remains of the two local hotels stood partially intact. They were the Continental and the Hotel des Roses. In better times, they had been populated by pilgrims coming to the Monastery. Now they were empty, and probably always would be.

In the weeks before this bombing, the weeks after the slaughter of Freyberg's New Zealand and Indian troops, there had been a lull in the fighting. New Zealand engineers had been managing to reconstruct some of the roads in the area. They had even managed to lay a few routes up toward the German fortifications.

Freyberg's plan—now that the town had been "fumigated"—was to use those routes to start rolling heavy materials up toward the Massif where the Monastery had stood, then across the Massif and beyond, to completely surround the German emplacements, then back onto a newly repaired Route 6, all the way to Rome and beyond.

***

As the Kiwis walked through the steaming remains of the town, they each shared a bit of contentment that a plan had finally worked as plotted, but too much devastation surrounded them for there to be any real celebration. Yet—finally, *finally,* something had worked out. It had taken a thousand truckloads of bombs, but one area at least—this little dead town—had been "softened up" by bombs. Carpet bombing had worked this time. German resistance was gone. No Germans had been spotted retreating to the hills, so they were all dead. The town belonged to the victors.

Then the Kiwis heard a single popping sound.

Then another.

It was a sound they had heard a hundred times before, yet they refused to believe it.

Sniper fire.

The German paratroopers had survived the bombing; they were still defending the town.

***

Chapter Eleven:
Gli Sfortunati

"The Land of Labor and the Land of Rest,
Where mediaeval towns are white on all
The hillsides, and where every mountain's crest
Is an Etrurian or a Roman wall."

-from "Monte Cassino, Terra di lavoro"
by Henry Wadsworth Longfellow 1875

***

Gravity: that force which causes material bodies to be inexorably drawn toward the center of the earth.

It was gravity that had sucked all of those bombs out of the B-17 bomb-bay doors and then hurled them downward, first at the Monastery, then at the unsuspecting village for three and a half hours. And who was to know that the bombs wouldn't make it all the way to the center of the earth, but rather would explode on impact because the ancient and peaceful town of Cassino had foolishly gotten in the way of their downward path?

Those dim-witted military egomaniacs—with blood dripping from the corners of their greedy and self-serving mouths—weren't the problem. The fault was gravity, the force which causes material bodies to be drawn relentlessly toward the earth's core.

To put into somewhat more technical terms: Shit flows downhill.

Follow the analogy then: If shit flows downhill, where does it finally end up? Where does it stop, come to rest? Who gets covered with it in the end?

The High Command? No, they might catch some crap when they mess up a campaign, when they blow call after call, when they allow their egomania to get in the way of common sense and good military strategy, when they try to balance black ink with black death and end up with the death winning—while resting easy in the knowledge that any death incurred would be somebody else's, somebody below them, somebody lower down.

No, the Generals would not be the ultimate shit receptacle.

The midlevel officers? No, these guys often suffered and died shoulder-to-shoulder with their men, but they were recognized as necessary and valuable cogs in the war machine. Shit would certainly wash over them and theirs in these difficult days, staining their uniforms and faces and souls, but the bad stuff would keep on flowing south.

So—who then? Who in the end would be graced with the title, "Ultimate Receptacle of all this Shit"?

The non-com maybe? The enlisted man?

***

Mack: Got my vote. It was us all right.

***

No, there were those residing even lower on the sliding scale of shit.

***

Scooter: Who? The monks maybe?

***

At least the monks had God on their side. As the military thought *they* did. But nobody wants to fuck up a monk's life. Could be hell to pay.

***

Mack: The mules.

***

Nope. The mules were considered a prized possession. Sure, they were being slaughtered at an absurd and abusive rate—cut down by machinegun fire, blown into bloody chunks of mule-flesh by the land mines, blasted by artillery, sent screaming to their deaths, fully loaded, over the edge of the cliffs—but these animals were *valued.* They performed a function, did a duty, got a job done that was absolutely necessary for the war effort. They were expendable, but not disposable. As a result, they were fed, watered, cared for, as best as the situation would allow. That genius General of the mountains, the Frenchman Juin, always made sure his mules were taken care of as well as possible under these conditions. Cared for as well as his men, whenever possible.

So then, who was of no worth to anyone? Who lived at the bottom of that hollow and polluted tank? Who could be labeled as "Ultimate Receptacle of All of the Shit of This War"?

***

Scooter: The peasants.

***

The peasants.

Other than the few mule handlers among them, the peasants were of no use to anyone, merely flotsam and jetsam, something to get in the way—and they were treated accordingly. Nearly all of the able bodied men, even if they were no longer really able bodied, had been conscripted by the Germans and sent off to God-knows-where to do Fuehrer-knows-what.

Those who remained were the sickly, the weak, the old, the frail, the tired, the dumb, the stunned, the insane, the terrified, the confused, and the children.

And that is exactly where the ultimate shit ultimately settled.

***

Since these were Italians citizens who were being bastardized, let's call them by a bastardized Italian phrase. Let's call them *Gli Sfortunati.* The Unlucky. What a difference an "S" makes.

Picture yourself enclosed within a box. To your left are the Apennine Mountains with their impenetrable walls of granite and limestone. Can't run that way. To your right, the Tyrrhenian Sea. No escape in that direction. In front of you is an advancing army of a dozen different countries; an army that will kill you; they've done it before. Behind you, another army, even worse, those who would also kill you without pause. Beneath your feet, land mines, anxious to explode. Above you, maybe worst of all, the airplanes, dropping death.

And this box's walls are closing in.

***

Part One: *Gli Sfortunati* are threatened

When this war came to Italy, July of 1940, (there had been many others) for the most part *Gli Sfortunati* were unimpressed and a bit confused, simply resigned. This was the way shit flowed. Mussolini was calling their men into military service; most went, some made plans to flee. The big Italian heart was never completely behind Mussolini or this war. Eventually the Italian army chalked up over thirty-five thousand deserters, leading the league in that category.

Although simple and for the most part uneducated, the common people were much smarter than their Fascist leaders in Rome. They knew this much: This war would be lost. It took the Fascists a few years to realize this fact; it took the Germans even longer, but *Gli Sfortunati* knew right away. Italy, then Germany, would lose.

They also knew that it really didn't matter—no matter who won or lost, the people in the fields and the streets would lose.

Their simple hope was that the war would not hugely impact them; maybe it would pass them by as quickly and painlessly as possible. When it became obvious that the Allies would decide on a southern strategy—that they would invade the toe of the boot and then head up the calf—*Gli Sfortunati* hoped that the advance would be swift, sure, and mostly harmless to their way of life. Break out the American flags for a morning or two, wave and smile at the Yanks, lock up your daughters, grab some chocolates from the smiling soldiers, and be done with it.

But the old men already knew. The old men had seen the First World War. If this one was to be anything like that one, and it would be, there would be hell to pay.

Fascism had always had a stronger hold on the people of the north than it did down here, but still, the kids would proudly don the black suits and toy rifles of the Fascist Youth. The kids didn't have the fervor of their young counterparts in Berlin, but still, to any kid a flashy uniform is a flashy uniform and a toy rifle is a gun. Let's go out and play.

As the war progressed, Mussolini started demanding that the people turn in any valuable heirlooms—wedding rings, maybe a bracelet from a deceased aunt or the chalice from the town church. *Gli Sfortunati* did what they were asked to do—people like this always do—but gradually the thought crept through the town that this would not be the end of it. Things would get worse, much worse. They would have much more than their jewelry and possessions taken from them.

***

Part Two: *Gli Sfortunati* are displaced

The Germans in occupied European cities would often raid a restaurant or social club, round up thirty or forty men, and send them to slave labor camps.

During the course of the war in southern Italy, eventually every citizen of the town of Cassino was made homeless. Some managed to get to relatives in surrounding towns and villages, a few with overseas connections actually managed to get out of the country. But most hovered in the Cassino area, some in open fields, some in caves, some even in those tiny abandoned rock towers that the soldiers had built for shelters—the sangars. We have already seen that hundreds of the locals sought shelter in the Monastery, where the monks were not overjoyed to see them.

Sometimes the armies would use whips and clubs to drive the commoners from one location to another; at other times the Germans told them they would be machinegunned if they tried to move. And sometimes they were.

When these people were forced to leave one spot under threat of artillery, they would try to hold large bed sheets above their heads—to act as a white flag. Pilots and artillery gunners sometimes managed to convince themselves that the sheets were just someone's laundry, and they would drop their bombs and fire their shells anyway. In an area streaked over with grays and browns, white spots can make good targets.

***

Part Three: *Gli Sfortunati* are hit with bombs and artillery

Sometimes the dead would be listed as "collateral damage," just accidental casualties of the war; sometimes they would be the intended target. Hurts just as bad either way.

For the citizens of Cassino, the first sight of death from above came early, in July, 1943, when B-17's dropped bombs on the airfield at Aquino, just a few miles away. Here was the war firsthand. Some townspeople grew concerned about stray bombs (they still did not believe that they themselves could be targeted), and so they moved out into the countryside. There they would be displaced but alive. Their children would see 1944.

Early in the war, the Army Air Corps was committed to "strategic bombing" that would only hit military targets and production areas. The mass bombing of civilians and civilian targets was something that only beasts like the Germans would resort to, as they had in Poland and Spain and wherever they felt it necessary. For awhile the American press kept alive the idea that Americans would not stoop to such atrocity. American magazines and newspapers would boast about the incredible accuracy of the bombing raids. Their reports made it seem that if a munitions factory stood between a school and a hospital, the factory could be taken out with surgical precision. It couldn't.

The idea of clean bombing did not stick around for long. By the war's end, we would take Germany's lead and our bombs would kill many more civilians than combatants. All over Europe.

Back in America, well-intentioned groups like "The Council of Learned Societies" and "The American Commission for the Protection and Salvage of Artistic and Historic Monuments" would pressure the government to spare museums and art centers and monuments and architectural masterpieces. Protecting innocent civilians was not part of their agenda. *Gli Sfortunati* would fend for themselves.

***

Mack: Besides, by the time someone got done saying "American Commission for the Protection and Salvage of Artistic and Historic Monuments," the bombs had already been released.
Scooter: How'd you remember that whole thing?
Mack: I've lost my innocence, not my memory.
Scooter: Mmm.
Mack: Sometimes I wish I'd lost both.

***

Sometimes the Allies would bomb with good intentions but bad results. In Naples, one point three million people were doused from the sky with a remedy meant to combat the typhus that was killing the city. But the remedy they used was DDT.

***

Part Four: *Gli Sfortunati* are robbed

Never mind Himmler and his swag and his ill-gotten goods and the Nazis' penchant for looting art treasures from whatever country they conquered. Artifacts were swell, but *Gli Sfortunati* were more interested in supper—food that was taken from their table. If they had a table. The Germans, and later the Allies, robbed their farms of sheep, lambs, and cows. Food.

Throughout the war, *Gli Sfortunati* remained incredibly generous to the troops, always willing to share whatever they could with the young men who had come to "liberate" them.

Sometimes the young soldiers would reciprocate; often they would not.

Once in awhile the Germans and Allies would toss a few *lire* as they left the people to starve; the money rarely came close to the actual value of what was taken. And you can't eat money, either paper or coin.

This is what happened to the monks' livestock when the Monastery was being evacuated. Many villagers remained and would not evacuate, you might remember, because they were either too sick and wounded to travel, or their children were, or they rightfully feared that they would be slaughtered on the road leading out of the Abbey (even with their white laundry flag flapping). So they stayed huddled within the walls of the Monastery and watched their food being led away.

One of a thousand incidents: An Italian family trying to remove itself from harm's way came upon some Moroccan troops (our side) on the road. The family had made the mistake of having some polenta (corn meal) and olive oil with them. Not the makings of a sumptuous feast, but enough food to survive on. The Moroccans decided a snack of polenta and olive oil would hit the spot.

The soldiers were fought off by the elderly grandmother of the group, who swung her walking stick at them each time they started grabbing for the food. The soldiers had their weapons, grenades and rifles, but decided that the old woman was nuts and it wasn't worth a killing or taking a shot to the side of the head with a walking stick.

Peacetime, wartime, don't ever stand between an old Italian *goo-mah* and her polenta.

***

Part Five: *Gli Sfortunati* are starved to death

The plague of hunger spread across Cassino in progressively darkening stages.

At first there was rationing, beginning with salt, then sugar and butter, then olive oil, meats and wheat. The bread turned black, the pasta turned into mystery dough, the meats disappeared altogether. As universally happens under these conditions, a Black Market immediately sprang up. For the right price, and by knowing the right Fascist officer, a *Sfortunata* mother could still secure something edible for her children. For the right price, the payment coming from either in her purse or between her legs.

Nearly simultaneous with the rationing came the shortages. Same products, higher Black Market prices, then none to be had at all, no matter how many inflated *lire* bills you greased a palm with.

The next stop on the No-Gravy train was a gnawing hunger. Hunger should never come into play in an area like this—not here in farm country, a countryside of mostly fertile soil, good precipitation, three nearby rivers, and a hardworking and knowledgeable farming community. But war trumps all that.

Last stop, the ultimate terminal for this train—starvation. Statistics are spotty in this area, since sickness and starvation are often entwined, and nobody was performing autopsies or bothering to keep count. The medical men had more important tasks at hand; the others were too busy just trying to stay alive.

Malaria was rampant because of the Valley being flooded by the Germans, and because of the water being stuffed with the dead corpses of people and animals. A mosquito bite was not an annoyance any more, but rather a potential death sentence. A body weakened by hunger cannot fight off malaria. Does it really matter what the official cause of death is, especially when there *is* no official cause of death, and nobody would care anyway?

Whenever a German army—or any army—occupied a foreign country, it was understood that all food would first go toward feeding the soldiers. Not only had all incoming supplies to Italy ceased, but in occupied territories like Cassino, food was actually being shipped *out* of the area.

Back in Naples, the tropical fish of the Neapolitan Aquarium were de-tanked and eaten. The prize manatee was butchered and served to Petoola himself, who loved sea food. History does not record his reaction nor that of his digestive tract.

Six-year-old kids there in Naples resorted to stealing supplies first from the Germans, then from the Allies, and selling the swag on the Black Market. None of the kids had a wage-earner or breadwinner left in the family to care for them, nothing close to that. Only an empty stomach and a taste for survival.

Starving wasn't such a bad thing, the mothers of *Gli Sfortunati* finally decided. It was a feeling you could get yourself used to. It was an exit door from this hell. But watching your children starve to death, that was another thing, too heavy a cross for anyone. It would have been an impossible burden for the great Saint Benedict himself.

***

Part Six: *Gli Sfortunati* are maimed

We're not talking about body parts and limbs that were blown off innocent children by the indiscriminate bombing. We're not talking about the legs and genitals that were blown off kids by the indiscriminant landmines. Let's talk about face-to-face, *mano a mano* maiming.

Just a quick example:

As an Allied troop carrier rolled into town, the starving kids would reach under the tarp and try to steel whatever they could reach. They didn't know that a giggling soldier was hiding beneath the tarp with a ready bayonet, taking fingers as trophies.

***

Part Seven: *Gli Sfortunati* are wounded

Again, let's skip the obvious; you've heard enough about that.

Instead, this: One farmer tried to save the life of a young girl by amputating her leg using a pair of rusty scissors.

***

Part Eight: *Gli Sfortunati* are tortured

As horrible and inhumane as the physical torture of these poor people was, the mental torture was always far worse. Some physical wounds heal with time, most at least can be lived with.

But when a young person's mind is tortured, there is doubt that it will ever fully recover. How many survivors have been snapped back awake by a terrifying dream, years after the hostilities have ceased.

How much alcohol, how many drugs, would it take to snuff out the memories of this mass inhumanity?

***

Part Nine: *Gli Sfortunati* are raped

Back in Naples, for the fighting man on leave, women were cheap. The ladies would line up with a metal cup on the floor at their feet, coins accepted; they smiled and told the soldier boys that they could leave their boots on. *Quick and easy, Joe, no?* The clap became as common as a sneeze; the army replaced gumball machines with prophylactic dispensers.

Out in the war zone, women were even cheaper to get; they were free for the taking. *Way Marie, way Marie, tonight we get it for free.*

German soldiers would take a woman into custody claiming that she had stolen something, but their real reasons were too often too obvious.

When a division of Goumirs—Moroccan mountain troops—"liberated" the area, *Gli Sfortunati* thought their troubles would be over, or at least lessoned. Then the Goumirs reportedly started raping the woman at gunpoint. Some witnesses said that young girls were raped and raped again, and then again. Until they died.

Many old Italians insist that these French North Africans were the worst of the rapists—either fact or racial prejudice talking. But it is a fact that sometimes an Italian man had a choice to make: Stand by and watch your sister or mother be raped to death, or step forward into a bullet or a knife blade.

Old men and young boys could also become victims of this horny, sexual military onslaught.

Less animalistic soldiers would sit by, a few yards off, and hear the screams of the victims. *Should we do something? No, Lieutenant says just follow orders, don't be upset by it.*

Some female victims, who had the temerity not to die, were led off in straightjackets.

***

Part Ten: *Gli Sfortunati* are murdered

One hundred forty-eight skulls were found in the ruins of the bombed Monastery. None were monks, none were Germans.

As the Benedictines were getting ready for that Fellini-like procession down the mountain after the bombing, they checked on a group of three children. Their father had disappeared, their mother had been killed. The monks studied the three kids. On might be saved, so she was lifted up to be taken down the mountain. The other girl was so close to death that she would never survive the trip; she only had a few minutes to live, so she was left there. She died. The boy, their brother, had both his legs cut off during the attack. He screamed in pain when a monk tried to lift him, so he was also abandoned there, to die alone beside the body of his sister.

A few weeks earlier, on a clear afternoon before the Monastery had been destroyed, one of the monks happened to be looking out across the surrounding fields, perhaps imagining how beautiful the countryside had been before and, with God's help, would be again. His eye caught a slight movement in the ravine behind the Abbey. It was just a woman, with her two-year-old daughter. Maybe the woman too was thinking about better times to come.

But then American artillery caught sight of the movement; they tossed in a shell that killed the woman and blew a hole in the side of the child's head. When a rescuer managed to get the small body into the Monastery, brain tissue was leaking out. The body was still and lifeless. Cold.

Eighty-five thousand innocent Italian civilians were killed during the war. In some societies, under different circumstances, the killing of an innocent civilian—one who was threatening harm to no one—is considered murder.

***

Part Eleven: Finally, *Gli Sfortunati* are abandoned

Italy was given some Foreign Aid after the war, as most European countries were; the gesture did little and meant less to the Italians.

They simply wanted the armies to be gone.

The foreign armies had left a parting gift for *Gli Sfortunati*: A countryside holding a half million hidden and unexploded land mines.

***

Jim DeFilippi

"...Three!..."

Chapter Twelve:
The Fighting Turns Feral

"Gray mists were rolling, rising, vanishing;
The woodlands glistened with their jeweled crowns."

-from "Monte Cassino" by Henry Wadsworth Longfellow 1875

***

The New Zealand soldiers in Cassino town were stunned to find German paratroopers still alive and defending the place after the carpet bombing; then another realization hit the Kiwis: just like with the destruction of the Monastery weeks before, the bombardment of the town had produced the direct opposite effect of the one desired. The bombing had turned the town into a perfect site for staging a defensive holding action. Only a few Germans were left alive there, but those who were had a thousand spots in which to hide and from where to fire off their sniper bullets, machinegun shells, and *Panzarschreck* bazooka cartridges.

For the New Zealanders, this nowhere land of craters and smoking rubble had become a tripwire across the edge of an open grave.

Once again the Allies' superiority in tanks and armament and airpower had been neutralized by that Command's own stupid decision making. For the destruction of the town to have served any purpose at all, the bombardment would have had to have been followed immediately by the advance of the tanks—while German heads and bodies were still reeling and shaking from the bombing. But the bombing had so shredded the town infrastructure that the Allied tank commanders could not even find a passable road, could not even identify something as a route to take. Huge craters, confusion and those *Panzarschrecks* brought the tanks to a frustrating and stalled-out halt at the edge of town.

So once again the responsibility for an Allied advance fell onto the slumping shoulders of the exposed and exhausted infantryman. As the foot soldiers began to fight their way across town—against that stubborn and invisible enemy—the engineers got to work directly behind them, trying to clear a path for the tanks. Both groups provided ready targets for German fire.

Just like up on the Snake's Head Ridge earlier, the Germans were protecting a natural bottleneck. At a point near Route 6, the possible passage route for vehicles was narrow and singular, a perfect spot upon which to rain down artillery fire. The old "single file into death" scenario of the Ridge had been replaced with "single lane traffic into death."

In town, a Kiwi infantryman—pinned down by Germans fire—heard horrible screaming from somewhere beneath his feet. He realized that a German soldier was buried alive down there, crushed from the bombardment but still managing to breathe and to scream. Giving in to his own humanity, the Kiwi tried to dig down to rescue the enemy soldier, but each time he pulled a rock or chunk of cement off the pile, two more fell to take its place. Finally the noble rescuer stopped digging. All night the horrible subterranean screaming went on; in the morning, there was silence.

A hard rain began to fall and by dusk the troops were trying to slog their way through a paste of dust and water formed by the dirt of war meeting the moisture of nature. But poetry doesn't help when your boots are getting stuck and sucked down, and it's so dark you have to hold the flaps of the fatigue shirt of the man in front of you for guidance forward.

Give me light, give be light. The only available light was the brief killing sparks of the enemy's guns.

***

High above the town, New Zealanders, British, and Gurkhas were all trying to forge a path up to the Monastery ruins, but there too, chaos, darkness and confusion were controlling the scene.

A group of Gurkhas went off-communication for hours, only to reappear with no explanation of what had happened. These Gurkhas—these simple soldiers from Nepal—all came from a poverty stricken, uneducated background. Many of them had enlisted while not even knowing there was a war going on. To a man they were fierce and savage warriors. When soldiers from other nations saw a comrade fall, they would rush forward to lend aid. When a Gurkha saw a mate fall in battle, he would rush forward to grab his food.

A group of them came upon three sleeping Germans. They quietly beheaded two and left the one in the middle alone and undisturbed—the target of a morbid wakeup gag.

The Kiwi slang for a raw recruit was "red arse"; when the Gurkhas had arrived, no one had called them that.

***

The morass of horror proved to be too much for some of the men's psyche; at times a combination of psychosis and British reserve took over the tired soldier's mind. A proper British Major simply put down his weapon, left the fray, walked stiffly back to his command post, saluted, and quietly announced with his clipped British accent that he had lost his nerve. One wounded yet smart military man.

The fighting in the town was so congested, so insane, that one platoon of Brits actually shared a house with German paratroopers for a day and a half; the Brits living downstairs, eating K-rations and smoking the last of their cigarettes, while they could hear the thud of German jackboots above their heads on the second floor.

The Germans holding the town were gradually exterminated until they held total control of only the two hotels on the outskirts—the Continental and the Hotel del Roses. Neither place was currently offering room service.

Above, up on the Massif, the huge manpower superiority of the Allies had finally begun to take its toll on the outnumbered Germans; the Monastery ruins were gradually surrounded by advancing troops.

Freyberg and Petoola must have thought then that finally—*finally*—their team was about to bust through the vaulted Gustav line. Freyberg's unwarranted self-assurance matched Petoola's, pound for pound, delusion for delusion. Remember: Just like Petoola, when Freyberg's troops had been slaughtered in a nighttime raid, he had ordered them to attack again in the morning. This time at least, General Dimoline, the Indian, had managed to convince him that such an attack would prove to be even more futile and deadly than the ones that had gone before.

Freyberg led his Kiwis and Indians with a sloppy, impulsive bluster that was every bit as deadly as his American counterpart's. Freyberg was a big, strapping General who rarely gave up on a plan, no matter how unfeasible, especially if it was his own; before the war he had tried to swim the English Channel, twice, and had to be hauled exhausted from the sea both times, spitting out salt water like he was now spitting out attack orders.

British General Alexander had been named overall theater commander in southern Italy, but Freyberg and Petoola each had direct command of their armies. Now they were sure they had begun to see proof of what their superior military intelligence could achieve. The town of Cassino was nearly theirs, the ruins of what had been the Monastery was nearly surrounded, the bottleneck up to Rome was nearly cracked open. So now once again—at last—the rallying cry of these two egoists was: *Roma, Roma, here we come.*

***

Not so fast, soldier-boy.

Up until now, things had remained quite civilized. But everything was about to degenerate.

Those iron-willed Germans still weren't done for. Didn't they understand that they were fighting a hopeless skirmish in a hopeless battle in a hopeless theater in a hopeless war?

Still, they had been stubbornly hanging onto their positions and their territory, including the ruins of an ancient castle up on Castle Hill—an important stepping stone to Hangman's Hill, which was itself a stepping stone to the ruins of the Monastery, a stepping stone to Rome. Allied forces approaching Castle Hill were caught in a withering crossfire that was more intense than anything they had experienced so far.

The battle-within-a-battle for control of the ancient ruins of the Castle became the most feral, primal, combat of all of Monte Cassino.

Each time the Brits would manage to storm the Castle and gain control, the Germans would counterattack, again and again, until successful, climbing the walls like something out of a medieval combat manual. The Brits would be tossing their Mills grenades, the Germans their stick grenades. If a soldier of either side got to an enemy grenade before it detonated, he would toss it back from where it had come, then hide and hope.

One young man of the Essex brigade was huddled inside the Castle when a stick grenade landed at his feet. As he quickly grabbed the obscene thing and hurled it back outside, another landed in the same spot. As he threw the second one back, a third landed. He reached for that one too. Time had run out.

From this "Monkey in the Middle with Live Hand Grenades" game, the action degenerated even further. The fighting dissolved into hand-to-hand, face-to-face, rip off someone's ear, grab a lip and try to tear it loose before your fingers were bitten off—a 1950s street gang rumble gone rancid and atavistic.

Issued weapons: boots, bayonets, belts and buckles.

P.O.W.'s (Privately owned weapons): Billy clubs, brass knuckles, hunting knives, sharpened rocks, chunks of broken glass.

Feral.

The extermination of civilization.

***

Yet, during the same action, some inter-army camaraderie:

During a lull in the ferocious attacks and counter attacks, a British soldier decided, *What the hell*, and he simply strolled outside the walls of the Castle to retrieve the body of a comrade. This savior of a fallen friend might have been suffering from battle-brain damage, or maybe he had just come to his senses. Either way, the surprised Germans didn't fire on him. They simply watched with respect as the valiant young soldier grabbed his buddy's lifeless body to drag it back inside the Castle. At the Castle door, he turned and snapped off a salute to his enemies.

Some unintentional inter-army camaraderie:

American airplanes conducted a Food Drop to resupply the starving Brits and Gurkhas on the ridge, but the bundles of food fell on a German controlled area instead. Finally the term "Friendly Fire" had lived up to its name.

***

In the spirit of inter-army camaraderie, a short informal truce interrupted the killing—a ceasefire to let each side pick up its dead. This was a fairly common occurrence, not one that the command of either side was comfortable with, but something that neither side would risk denying the fighting man.

The mini-armistice coated the hillside with a silence too sad to be broken, as each side ventured out to pick up its fallen. Germans helped Englishmen to load and carry corpses; it didn't matter what uniform the dead man happened to be wearing.

Finally, some distant sniper fire from higher up on the mountain caused everyone to look over his shoulder, and the truce had ended.

***

The battle for the Castle was astonishing on both sides. At one point the Germans managed to place an explosive charge beneath one of the Castle walls. When the wall blew out, the Germans charged in, only to be met with a storm of machinegun fire. Of the two hundred that attacked, only forty paratroopers were left standing and managed to retreat.

The Brits holding the Castle were not fairing any better; losing man after man in a historically courageous action.

Instead of being congratulated for their *uber*-human effort, the men received a radio message from Command that irritably asked: "What's the hold-up up there? Why aren't you puffs advancing swiftly up the ridge toward the next high point, Hangman's Hill, as the Master Plan calls for?"

You simply cannot please some moron carrying lots of pretty stars on his shoulders and lots of reckless self-esteem within his chest.

***

The Germans still had control of the Continental Hotel, further down hill from the Castle. So there was no frontline, no clear cut idea of who controlled what, no sense of order anywhere. The Germans might be defending territory against an enemy coming *down* the hill at them, instead of up. The English might be twisting in circles, looking for the next attack.

Communication among different platoons and squads broke down until it became nearly nonexistent. Landline radio wires had been shredded, radios had been soaked in water, shelling by the British twenty-five pounders would drowned out all voices. It didn't matter—communication from Command would have been as soaked in stupidity as the radios were soaked in water and mud.

Sometimes *not* being able to hear from your leaders worked out well—at least for a brief time. A fleet of Allied tanks was supposed to advance as Hangman's Hill was being simultaneously attacked by the infantry. The infantry was not even close to launching their attack; they had been stopped at the Castle and hadn't even gained control of the hotel.

But nobody told the tank boys that; they figured their orders were still on, so they fired up the engines and moved out; the tanks advanced with amazing speed. The Germans couldn't believe what they were seeing. Tanks *always* came in conjunction with an infantry attack. Here were the tanks, but where was the infantry? Ultimately the tanks were turned back by German *Panzarschreck*—its design and action similar the American bazooka—but everyone agreed that if the infantry had been there to support the tanks, it would have been a major victory for the Allied troops.

***

By now even Freyberg had to admit that this latest plan had been a complete Chinese Fire Drill—with the firemen involved being his loyal boys and the fire being gunfire and the siren being the whale of a thousand lives wasted. The plan had called for Germans resistance in the razed town to have been destroyed before the attack had begun—especially the resistance around the Continental Hotel. This goal had not come close to being achieved.

A second part of the plan had been the advance of the Tank Corps up the hillside toward the Monastery. This had been successful for awhile, but lack of coordination with any infantry had doomed it. The tanks had been stopped. They had looked around, seen none of their infantry, and then retreated.

A third aim had been the taking of Hangman's Hill. This had been achieved finally, but the troops up there were now cut off, without supplies, water, food, or hope of reinforcement. The isolated soldiers resorted to getting water by sneaking down to a natural pool at night and filling up a load of canteens. It was only after the third night that they discovered the body of a dead mule lying in their water supply. The creature looked like it had been there at least three weeks.

These exhausted men had been conducting ancient hand-to-hand combat for night after night. They were stunned by battle fatigue and paralyzed by muscle fatigue. They no longer trusted their officers or anyone beyond an arm's length of where they were currently lying. Slowly, they had come to realize the futility of their efforts and of their sacrifices.

Even from his distant position—well behind the fighting—Freyberg could imagine the looks on their faces and the feelings in their hearts. Finally, he ordered an end to this attack. A volunteer snuck his dangerous way up to Hangman's Hill and led the weary men back down.

Then, stretcher bearers waving Red Cross flags and white banners began to clean up the mess.

Once again, the Allied commanders looked at the war map; it showed German positions virtually unchanged. Once again, the dead had died for nothing.

An Allied general, showing a rare display of intelligence and humanity, told his fellow officers that these men had lost more than a battle. They had lost their substance.

***

After this third failure to take Monte Cassino, a quiet settled over the Valley.

As H. W. Longfellow had written, those gray mists were rolling and rising, those woodlands were glistening. A brief but appreciated silence had come to Monte Cassino. And spring would soon be coming to the Valley.

The lull gave the Allied commanders a chance to ruminate on their many mistakes. First, they had tried to storm the area with American infantry. The men couldn't even get across the *Rapido* to get close to the target.

Then, the aerial destruction of the Monastery was supposed to soften up the German entrenchment enough so that the subsequent attack could be successful. But no subsequent attack had been readied. Even if it had, it would have been stopped dead in its tracks.

The Allied faith in its air power had remained unwavering. *If destroying the Monastery by air was not the answer, we'll destroy the town the same way.* And they did. And again got the same results.

Some great military minds after the war have suggested that this third attempt was undermined by Freyberg's not sending enough troops up the hills right after the bombing. Some great minds never tire of sacrificing other men's lives. The bottlenecks would still have been there. The soldiers would still be going single file. The German machineguns would still have enough ammunition to keep the shooting gallery open for the night.

***

A major reason that this third attack was even considered in the first place was to relieve the pressure on the troops landing at Anzio. It was hoped that the Germans would have to move so many men off the beaches to defend the Gustav line that the Cassino attack would prove valuable.

This was not the case. Before the third attack at Cassino had even begun, the Anzio beachhead, covered by shelling from artillery and naval vessels, had been firmly established. That old apologetic excuse used so often by retarded military minds—"Well, we lost a lot of good men but at least we forced the enemy to assign troop from somewheres else"—almost never makes sense. Our own men could have been used in that other place too.

That same wise General (no sarcasm this time) who had declared that his men had lost more than a battle, they had lost their substance, now just shook his head and marveled at the English insistence to always attack the enemy at his strongest point, rather than at the weakest.

Frido, the German leader who had marveled at the stupidity of destroying the Monastery, could not understand the reason for this third attack either. Why had it been planned and carried out at all? So much foolishness. So much slaughter, on both sides. More than one of Frido's fellow officers, and a few enlisted men, had voiced the same inconceivable wish: *All things considered, I'd rather be in Russia.*

***

A late winter snow tossed a blanket over the rotted land, covering the warm corpses and cold rock around Cassino. With the snow came the uneasy lull in the fighting. It was as if officers and fighting men on both sides had simply been bled too dry to go on slaughtering each other any longer. And so, for a brief time at least, they sat and breathed and tried to remember what living a normal life meant.

Here was a Mexican standoff between these naive Americans with their international pals and the Germans. In Italy. Without speaking any words, each side said to the other: *If you don't kill me for a little while, I won't kill you.*

It was by no means a return to everyday life, but it was something different from the feral fighting of the last months. Although the word "peace" was not even considered as a description of this situation, at least here was something, here was a brief, sporadic splotch of something resembling peace.

A respite from the incessant, ferocious fighting.

In some ways, it made things worse.

The break gave a man a chance to notice how he had been living during that winter. To look back at what he had done, what he had seen others do, and what was left for him now.

Absolute filth saturated everything. There was no way to keep any part of your body free from the Italian dirt or from the leaking rivulets of your own blood and conscience. Rats, vermin, fleas, ticks, and things without names hopped from one rotting body to the next, all around you, then onto your arm, your leg, your crotch and your chest. The vermin and the insects seemed to be enjoying this war, even if no one else was. Maybe war had been created for them, for the rats and the bugs.

Yet even some rats were killed in action. If you happened to be sitting there with your rifle or pistol handy, and one runs by, what else would you do but make it possible for the rodent to die for its country.

Sometimes, if you were encamped too close to a dead human/mule dumping ground, the smell was so bad that not even a tight-fitted gasmask could keep the scent away from your face. Some dead bodies became as much a part of the landscape as the granite and the burnt olive bushes.

One bloated and blackened corpse at the entrance of some abandoned pillbox became everyone's friend. At first the bloat of death pushed out his stomach like a jolly uncle's. A few days later it split his belt and ripped open his shirt and spilled itself all over his loins. Still, the gentle, almost smiling expression on his green face did not change.

A petrified hand of a dead French soldier—no one knew from what outfit—extended from a pile of dirt and rock. The fingers reached out into the air, as if in greeting, and the flesh never seemed to rot. Passing soldiers got into the habit of shaking the hand each time they slipped by. A bit of the gesture was for luck, a bit for a gag, and although they never admitted it, a bit for silent tribute. The hand remained warm to the touch, for days.

The smell of decaying flesh was not the strongest aroma. The worst was that of human shit; the smell of dysentery and diarrhea combined with the lack of any sanitary fixtures. When you're being shelled two or three times a day, or incessantly, sometimes you would have make the decision to let it dump right there in your own sangar. You knew you would regret it later on, but sometimes it was impossible to wait for a cessation in the fireworks or for night to fall.

Sporadically, bare asses could be seen lining up on hillsides when conditions seemed right. Asses as white as the snow, all in a row. Shit as brown as the dirt, falling in formation, like bombs.

If you were lucky, you didn't have to take a shit all that often, because you weren't eating all that much. K-rations might be available, potable water often was not. Dehydration led to aching throats and blistered lips.

The common foot soldier has an uncanny knack for finding and securing alcohol, and it was astounding how many of the battles were fought in a state of complete or partial drunkenness.

Booze, it was said, made it easier to live like this. Booze, it was known, made it easier to die.

The lull in the fighting—this strange intra-chapter of war—also gave men the chance to realize how lonely they were. A letter from home was a piece of magic, a respite from hell, something good, a thing that you could hold in your hand and press up to your mouth and nose and sleep with and read over and over again.

Some men wrote home constantly, incessantly, whenever they could.

***

Mack: John Ireland, in *Walk in the Sun,* was always composing his letter out loud. To his sister. To write down later. When he got a chance.
Scooter: You really liked that movie.
Mack: Was about southern Italy, '43, maybe '44. Filmed in Hollywood, I bet.
Scooter: Where they had that big sign, saying the name, up there on the hill, instead of a Monastery.
Mack: Wouldn't you like to see that thing get bombed?

***

The letters going back home were filled with pleas, quiet emotion, and false bravado: *Don't worry about me, I'm doing fine, be home soon.* Sometimes the words gave sanitized descriptions of the hell—either self-censored or censure-censored. Some suggested that everyone should follow Ira Gershwin's advice: *Let's call the whole thing off.* Not a bad idea.

Of course, no matter what your name was, the letter from home that you feared the most started with "Dear John." No one wanted to be two-timed from thousands of miles away. The German propaganda machine loved to play into this ubiquitous G.I. fear: *Hey, Johnny, what's your gal up to back home, while you're over here?* Leaflets and radio broadcasts from both sides tried to ruin the morale of the other. The Germans loved to quote FDR: As long as he was running things, Franklin had promised, no American boy will ever fight on foreign soil (as he was double dealing the country toward war).

For the most part, the propaganda was completely useless, ineffective, even silly. As if battle-hardened soldiers in the midst of all this would believe any officer's or politician's drivel. Yet the propaganda kept getting ground out and distributed. The boys in the propaganda outfits certainly preferred this duty—sitting in an office behind a typewriter—to sitting in a sangar beside a corpse.

***

This ragged excuse for life went on for awhile. Then the real spring came. The weather cleared, the air warmed. Finally, it was no longer necessary for an infantryman to piss on his rifle to defrost its mechanism.

The Generals looked out their windows and decided that the men had rested enough.

Fall in, fellas, time to get back to work.

***

Chapter Thirteen:
Hard Pretzels at the Alamo

"For, as the valley from its sleep awoke,
I saw the iron horses of the steam
Toss to the morning air their plumes of smoke,
And woke, as one awaketh from a dream."

-from "Monte Cassino" by Henry Wadsworth Longfellow 1875

***

    If history had unfolded differently, or simply been reported differently, these men might have been kings.

    I mean by that—the Kraut paratroopers.

    Let's say that somewhere along the line—that long supply line to the Russian Front—Uncle Joe Stalin and Hitler had sat down together and Hitler had said, "Look, this is ridiculous. We both want to be insane dictators of the entire world, but there's plenty world to go around. What say we stop all this foolishness, pool our resources, keep humoring *Il Douche-bag* for awhile, slay him, and then just sit back to enjoy our conquests. What can they do? Censure us in the League of Nations? Not let us come to the Olympics? We'll have our own Olympics. Of course, we'd kick your ass. German athletes are the greatest in the world. We're almost like a master race."

"So you think you can compete with our Soviet weightlifters? Your weightlifters could not even lift our cases of steroids and human growth hormone."

Or—if it were Joe speaking that penultimate paragraph—the last few sentence would read, "Our Soviet athletes are the greatest in the world. We're almost like a super race."

"You think you could beat our German women's track team? They have been so modified that one cannot even tell they are women. They run fast."

***

Mack: That all changed with Katarina Witt. Oh, I can see her sweet little can right now.

***

What I mean to say is this: If the Soviets and the Germans had signed a nonaggression pact, or if a hundred other things that didn't happen had happened—or that did happen hadn't happened—then the Germans would have won the war, and their stand at Monte Cassino would have lived on as their Alamo. TV shows, books, movies, all of them about the brave stand of a handful of soldiers.

***

Mack: You're full of shit. The U.S. would have never lost that war no matter what. We had the air power, we had the industry, we had guys like me and the Scooter fighting for us.

***

I know when not to argue. Okay then, let's take a different approach. Suppose my great-great-grandfather, Rudolf Heinrich Grif, had decided to stay put in his little cottage in the Black Forest years ago, instead of coming to America.

***

Mack: So?

***

So now I'm a German writing this book, this story of Monte Cassino. And it gets us back to the same place—I would be writing an account of the incredibly brave and noble soldiers of the German Paratrooper Corps.

***

Mack: I didn't know you were German. Explains a lot.

***

But you see my point.

***

Mack: Scooter, you're just sitting there, what do you think?
Scooter: No, not a whole book. I don't think you should be writing a whole book abut them. But sure, give them a chapter...

***

The First Parachute Division of the German Army had already distinguished itself as one of the toughest fighting forces in the world, even before they had hunkered down on the hills around the Monastery above Monte Cassino.

Early in the war, from as far north as Norway and as far south as Crete, they had gained the reputation of being able to drop into a precarious situation—drop out of the sky, clean up the mess by nightfall, and head off—Lone Ranger style—to the next problem.

They were all volunteers; their training had been long and difficult. And effective. The military discipline in their boot camp could be brutal. A young trooper accused of stealing was stripped, whipped, and thrown into a freezing room, until his screams could be heard around the base. This was no Article 15, and he wasn't screaming for a lawyer.

After the paratroopers had suffered huge casualties in Crete, Hitler had broken them down into smaller units, to be used selectively—to plug up holes in Russia, then to fight strategic battles in France, then to finally be shipped south to stem the tide in Sicily. Wherever the Reich had a dirty job that needed doing, these guys would be the ones called upon to do it. And they always did.

In Sicily, they had cleverly timed their appearance to avoid the superior fire power of the Royal Air Force.

It's never an easy day when you're a paratrooper for a team that is being out-gunned and out-flown by the other side.

***

One paratrooper told the story of jumping into a combat area as enemy antiaircraft artillery began firing up at them. Suddenly his buddies to the left and right were rocketing back up into the sky, blasting out of harm's way, as if they had jetpacks strapped to their chute packs.

"How are they doing that?" the young trooper asked himself. "They never taught *me* that trick in Jump School."

Finally, after a few more fellow jumpers had been rocketed skyward, he realized: "Wait a minute, they're not going up, I'm falling."

A shell had taken out his parachute. Quick thinking (well, not *too* quick) and his reserve chute allowed him to live to tell the tale.

***

Once on the ground and dug in at Monte Cassino, the German paratroopers realized that this fight would be a thousand-fold more difficult than anything else they had been through. Hitler decreed that any trooper who spent even a fortnight at Monte Cassino would receive the Iron Cross. Two weeks and you get a medal? What about those who served there two *months*? What about an entire *winter*? They don't make medals that impressive, haven't been invented yet.

Even before Monte Cassino, before Italy, the Division had fought so viciously and violently that they had achieved a reputation as thugs among the German people. When one young pilot from Berlin put in a request to cross-train to the paratroopers, the brass found that so absurd that they sent him to see a psychiatrist. The H-shrinker asked him why a pilot would want to give up his wings to join a group of gangsters on the ground. The young man told him, "I want to be in the war, not above it. I want to be a part of the bravest fighting group in Germany, in the entire world."

The shrink just looked at him, shrugged, scribbled down a few notes, and cleared him for paratrooper duty. *When will they ever learn?*

As the young troop was leaving his office, the doctor told him to make sure he didn't piss his pants in battle. And keep a tight asshole.

Another young future paratrooper was on a train, about to join up with his unit for the first time, when he told a stranger sitting across from him where he was going and what unit he was joining.

"Oh really?" was the reply. "So then, you've already killed your mother and your father?"

These German boys, walking that young man's tightrope strung between love of country/battle and a foolish belief in their own invincibility and immortality, became the men that the Allied troops had to face at Monte Cassino.

Their stubborn, borderline-insane bravery is even more impressive—even more hard to believe—when factored in with the unspoken truth with which most of them lived: Their cause was hopeless, their war was lost.

After Stalingrad, the entire world—many Germans included—could see that the all-powerful orange juice squeezer of the U.S. on one side and Russia on the other had the fruit of the Fatherland in its grip. It was simply a matter of time before the jaws would press and crush them east and west, even south. The juice machine would ultimately turn into a butcher shop, and they were to be a slab of meat.

As each Monte Cassino German paratrooper hung onto his filthy, stinking piece of earth—for week after week, month after month, against superior firepower, armament, airpower, and manpower—he knew in his heart that it was all for nothing. All for nothing. All for the foolish world vision of a paper-hanging madman with a loud voice and a mustache.

But the trooper hung on anyway.

***

They had bent down, fallen to their knees, held onto their helmets with one hand, to their buddies with the other, and survived the brutal bombing in and around the Monastery. When the Allied infantry finally began a trip up the mountain, the paratroopers had popped up their heads and announced, "Surprise, we're still here."

After they had done the same in the cellars of the buildings down in town—this time being the target of one of the most massive bombing attacks in the history of the world—all of it centered on a town the size of a couple city blocks—they had done the same, popped up again. "Yup, it's still us. We're still here."

Both the Allied Command and the Allied fighting man were incensed but impressed. General Alexander announced that he couldn't believe that *any* other soldier, including his own, could have lasted through what these young Germans were lasting through. And when it was done, when the B-17's had emptied their stomachs and gone home, did these men come out crying? ...throwing down their weapons? ...lifting their hands to the air? No. They came out firing.

General Alex declared them to be the best fighting men in the world, and they weren't even on his side.

A New Zealander wondered if even his beloved Kiwi troops could have stood up to what these Germans were standing up to. And a Kiwi is so tough he can stand up to anything.

The Allies' propaganda machine had a difficult time spinning the bravery of these men. The only tack they could take was: These people are zombies, willing to die for the madman Hitler.

But they weren't. They weren't zombies and they weren't dying for Hitler. Each paratrooper was dying for the guy next to him. Dying with some sense of camaraderie and pride in one's unit, in one's self. Misguided? Certainly. Insane? Maybe. Justified? No. But loyalty to that silly little mutt with the tiny mustache had little to do with any of what was happening.

***

Kurt Vonnegut—who had witnessed the brutality of this war close-up, and had lived to write about it, said, "We were empty-headed children in that war, as all ground soldiers are…And one idea that was put into our heads was that our enemies were so awful, so evil, that we, by contrast, must be remarkably pure."

***

Back in Berlin, the paratroopers' resolve and bravery was the only cause of celebration that the Reich Boys could come up with. But even this—their single item of good news—didn't give them any real reason for hope, only for pride. Foolish pride.

Adolph's Generals tried to kill him, but failed.

***

The lull in the fighting in the late winter of 1944 gave the German paratrooper time to review just how subhuman his existence had become. The Brits and Yanks were surviving horrors that the world had rarely seen, but he, the *Fallschirmjäger*, had it even worse.

The Yank could look behind him to the south, to the cheap wine and loose women of Naples; then look ahead to a victory party in Times Square. The German could look behind to a Rome that wanted him dead and gone; forward to a homeland infested by gloating American or Russian troops and German war crime trials.

The Germans spent the winter within bombed-out craters and smoky rock piles. Even the rats and the fleas and the corpses of his comrades seemed to know who would win. The Italian snow began to fall. *Oh, to be back once again in jolly Russia.*

Staying supplied with sufficient ammunition, food, and especially water was impossible. The paratroopers had control of the high ground, but their enemies had the air above. Their flimsy supply routes were closely watched and routinely fired upon. Men and mules died trying to make short, quick trips up and down the path that came to be known as Death Ravine.

I suppose that a mule cannot be referred to as "brave," but simply stubborn and stupid. Many of the animals would catch chunks of shrapnel in their side, legs and heads, but continue on with their job of getting supplies to their masters. The masters that were as stubborn as they were.

The phosphorous from the plate mines that the mules and men were carrying would often explode from the impact of a hit. The chemical would ignite and burn its way into the mule's hide and man's skin, almost impossible to remove until it had burned itself out. Friendly fire, close-up.

Somehow, with water, meals and military supplies nearly nonexistent, the liquor supply never quite ran out. A bewildering testament to a man and his *schnapps.*

***

Absurdly, Petoola's pride and joy—his Fifth Army Combat Propaganda Team—insisted that if bombs and bullets and starvation would not defeat these obstinate Krauts, then the only hope had to be—leaflets.

The P.R. Unit had a huge, portable printing press mounted on the back of a captured German tank carrier. Day after day the wordsmiths would turn out copy, and the press would produce pamphlets telling the Germans that the Allied attack was proving to be a huge success (even when this was not always true—military misinformation? Shocking!), and suggesting that the German soldier should look back over his shoulder for enemy troops coming down from the north.

American planes dropped load after load of exploding canisters on these Germans; but the canisters were not filled with gunpowder or shrapnel this time, they were filled with leaflets. This project was actually welcomed by the Germans, because when you are suffering from amoebic dysentery—which invariably leads to the physical function known as "salamander shits"—well then, leaves of grass act as a lousy ass-wiping tool. Especially if you are crouched out in the open, moving your bowels as quickly as you can, because you hear American planes approaching.

You know what's better than grass and leaves? Leaflets. A bit thick maybe, a bit rough, but a rather fine tool for the job.

They also used the American paper to dress wounds when their medical supplies ran out.

***

Even as they lived like subterranean rats through this historic hecatomb, the paratroopers could show amazing traits, traits greater than incredible loyalty and bravery. They could also somehow find it in their hearts to show at times—compassion.

These Germans maintained a basic humanity at their core—no matter what they were going through. It allowed them to treat a wounded enemy as well as they would treat their own.

During a lull after the third battle, an Allied stretcher crew had been sent out to collect the dead and dying. They happened upon a group of their own—four Kiwis and a Brit who were not only severely wounded but also incredibly drunk. Some rum had been airlifted in and they had retrieved it and put it to good use. As they were being carried down the mountain, they were intercepted by a German soldier carrying a Red Flag. The entire group was escorted to the German Commandant, who bummed a cigarette, probably tried to snag some of the un-devoured rum, saluted the bravery of *all* soldiers, and then let the crew go merrily on their way, back to their field hospital and to their hangovers.

Something there is among men who have suffered together, even if they have suffered on opposite sides; it might be based on the understanding that no one else could ever understand what they have been through, what they have been asked to do.

It's been said that prizefighters do not hate the man in the opposite corner. They know what he has suffered to get here, what sacrifices he has made. They know of the pain that accompanies him each time in that ring.

***

Scooter: My brother was in the ring. He told me the fighters only hate the civilians. The promoters and the managers and the leeches. All those who make money off their blood.

***

So then, can you understand my take on this, see my point? At the Battle of the Alamo, Davy Crocket and Jim Bowie and

William Travis and about one hundred men had held out for thirteen days against overwhelming odds. They were basically stealing the land they were fighting on, but they went on to be honored by books and history lectures and ever a cheesy movie by John Wayne.

The Germans at Monte Cassino had held out for a lot more than thirteen days. The odds against them were a lot more overwhelming than what the Texans were facing. They…

***

Mack: Yeah, yeah, but I somehow doubt we could get the Duke to make a glorious movie about these pretzels.

***

These pretzels were human. Religious, eccentric, devoted—and human. Their general Frido had actually been a lay Benedictine before the war; he always carried a love and respect for the monks and for the Italian people. And for his enemy.

A fellow general of Frido's—with the bad-ass name of Baade, General Baade—could have been lifted from a Marx Brothers movie. He wore Scottish kilts with his uniform and kept a monks' cowl hidden away for a disguise, in case he ever had to escape capture. He even kept a red dress for his aide to wear, for the same purpose.

***

Mack: Didn't that aide date J. Edgar Hoover for awhile?

***

These *Fallschirmjäger,* these "Green Devils" of Germany, had withstood combined artillery and bombing attacks that were unequaled in ferocity in the history of man. They had withstood hunger and thirst and numbing exhaustion. They had seen their numbers fall but yet they grow stronger as each friend dropped beside them. They had withstood the suicidal attacks of the best-equipped troops of the world—attacks from a dozen different nations, each throwing all of its firepower and manpower at these overwhelmed but never retreating Germans.

So what else could be done?

How could these immovable Germans Supermen ever be pushed off that mountain, ever be vanquished?

…well…well now… let's see… how about we send up a bunch of drunken Polacks at them?

***

"...Four!..."

Chapter Fourteen:
A Victory Sweet, Hollow, and Slightly Drunk

"Till in its cavernous chimney the wood-fire
Had burned its heart out like an anchorite."

-from "Monte Cassino" by Henry Wadsworth Longfellow 1875

***

As the horrible winter of 1943-1944 dribbled its way into spring, the insidious truth that most German troops had been trying to quell—that the war was lost, that they were dead men fighting—now became as bloated and green as a corpse, and then it ripened into this new horror: this singular fight to defend Monte Cassino was also a hopeless cause. The enemy was not going away, ever. They would use their superiority in everything but bravery to simply keep killing German soldiers. And if men kept dying, eventually the number of men left alive would be zero.

***

By May, as the weather was warming and drying out the Valley, the aggressors were planning the final destruction of

German troops in and around Monte Cassino. This time they managed to camouflage their intentions pretty well. Through trickery and deceit, they managed to convince the German Command that the beaches of Anzio were the real game, their real target. Both sides knew that the Allies' ultimate hope would be to crush the entire German Tenth Army between the forces that had landed at Anzio and the ground troops that had been fighting so long at the Gustav Line. The Anzio troops would be the hammer, the Monte Cassino troops simply a stationary anvil.

But by now Petoola and his English boss Alexander had suffered too many indignities to be satisfied with simply being an anvil; they were intent on crushing every last inland German. This time, they decided, the attack would not be made up of just two or three isolated offensives; instead it would be a mass campaign, throwing absolutely everything they could at these stubborn Kraut paratroopers.

The Allies would attack the mountains and the ridge and the rivers, all at once, each at multiple points. They would assemble enough men and equipment to leave no doubts.

Preparation. First, they brought in more troops—fresher, rested, and ready. Then they brought in more troops. Finally, they brought in more troops.

**

Mack: Did they increase the number of troops at all?

**

A huge mass of new Americans, mostly from New England, arrived. More Brits in various different divisions were made ready for this final assault. More Canadians, more New Zealanders, Indians, North Africans, Brazilians…

***

Mack: What, no Eskimos?

***

Over a hundred battalions. Ready to take a little hill in Italy's farm country. There were more than three Allied soldiers for every German, and that was counting dead Germans.

And the Allies had the machines. Some were already there, more were brought in. Finally assembled: two thousand tanks…three thousand airplanes…sixteen hundred large guns.

All this against a force that had already been decimated and basically was nothing but a band of ragged foot soldiers. Tired men with very few planes, fewer tanks. Little water and food, dwindling medical supplies and ammunition.

Sometimes an army can defeat an enemy solely by the use of sound strategy and well-utilized intelligence. But the only way to *annihilate* an enemy is with numbers. More and more, bigger and bigger, machines and divisions.

The scorecard for this final assault, this "Operation Diadem":

Big Guns: Allies—1600, Germans—45;
Tanks: Allies—2000, Germans 57;
Aircraft: Allies—3000, Germans 85;

Battalions: Allies—108, Germans 57 (and each at half the size).

No need to do any math.

***

In this same war, halfway around the world, Japan was fighting China, and each day China was losing thousands and thousands of men to the relatively few Japanese casualties. Each night, the satisfied Chinese Generals would just grin and tell each other, "Pretty soon, no more Japanese."

Back in Europe, no matter what happened, the last German would die while the last Allied soldier still lacing up his boots in Basic Training.

***

By now nothing about these assaults made much sense, if anything ever had. The idea of tying up German troops so that they couldn't be positioned on the French coast or the Anzio beach or anywhere else—was ludicrous.

On the eleventh hour of the eleventh day of the eleventh month, the last World War had ended.

Now, on May 11, at exactly 11 p.m., the full mass attack on Monte Cassino would begin.

On the days prior to this Eleventh of the Eleventh, tensions among the readying Allied troops mounted and festered. They were not told the specifics of what was to come, but a foot soldier can tell when he is about to be sent into the line of fire. They saw the crates of duck board being unloaded. The tons of Bailey Bridge elements.

In Petoola's Fifth, an enlisted man from New York reported that among the Blue Devils the cooks were jittery and the infantrymen were scared shitless.

***

Mack: That might've been me. I might've been me said that.

***

More and more desperate men began shooting themselves in various appendages, choosing self-mutilation over combat.

***

Mack: Smart guys.

***

Engineers were trying to clandestinely clear paths through the minefields; then trying to subtly mark the safe way forward. They were planning and preparing sites where Bailey Bridges could be quickly erected across the *Rapido* and its companion rivers. At night swimmers with measuring tapes would cross these rivers and then report back with distances, currents, and even water temperatures.

The sixteen hundred big guns were loaded and ready to saturate the enemy position. The fleet of heavy tanks was gassed up and ready to move, as soon as the Bailey Bridges had been erected. The aircraft had cleared their pre-flights and were ready to take off, their bellies bloated with bombs.

The huge multinational force was poised to strike. Like the beginning of a marathon, the "runners" were packed together, checking their watches, breathing deeply, jittery and wondering how they would perform, would they be there at the end.

British Fusiliers and Grenadiers, Lancers and the Black Watch, Light Infantry from Surrey and Kent and the Hampshires and Wales, Indian Gurkhas and riflemen, Punjabs and more light infantry. Canadian Armored and Infantry Brigades from British Columbia to the Maritime Provinces. Blue Devils. Americans from all forty-eight states. Moroccans, Algerians, Goumires. Juin's Frenchmen in the mountains with their plans and ammo and attitude.

***

Mack: Again may I ask, where the hell were the Eskimos in all of this?

Scooter: And midgets, how about midgets?

***

Of all the nations—all these varied young men from places all over the globe—the ones chosen to perform the most difficult task, to battle their way across the Cassino Massif and to take the Monastery ruins itself, to hoist their flag above the *Liri* Valley, was the fighting men that the other countries referred to as the "Bohunks."

The Poles.

There could not have been a better choice.

***

The Third Carpathian Rifles and Fifth Infantry Division of the Polish Corps, backed up by their Second Armored Brigade, under the command of their General Anders.

Few fighting forces anywhere could match the Bohunks in ferocity and bravery, and the only people they hated worse than the Russians were the Germans. True—they had been cornered and conquered and displaced and killed by Stalin. True—millions of their countrymen had been shipped to Siberia, to starve and be executed. True…the Russians had taken their lives and loved ones. All this was certainly true, but… the Germans would take their country. If Hitler won, there would be no Poland. Unacceptable.

To a man these Poles had learned to survive and they knew how to kill—no, how to massacre. Surprisingly, to their comrades from the other countries, they appeared to be especially civilized and sophisticated young chaps. Knew how to treat the ladies, smoked cigarettes from long FDR-like holders, would learn the language of whatever country they found themselves in. But they also knew how to fight and how to die, and they knew that in a few days that is exactly what they would be doing as they moved across the mountain rim toward the ruins of that Monastery.

These men knew how to hate and how to kill Germans. They would be fearless and vicious and brave. And some reports said that they would also be drunk. Being the fighting men that they were, they had their alcohol supply and they knew what to do with it. Even their mascot, a six-foot high, five hundred pound bear named Voytek—who had been used to carry heavy mortar rounds up the paths at Monte Cassino—enjoyed his evening glass of beer.

Enterprising soldiers had found that lemon juice could be distilled, that bad wine could be stomached, that vermouth and brandy were rare but could occasionally be liberated.

This ruin of a Monastery, this holy place at Monte Cassino—the Poles vowed—would finally be taken by a band of jug-fogged Bohunks.

***

It was nearly the eleventh hour of that eleventh day; fear was saturating the waiting men, a fear that was filling their lungs and their hearts and emptying their bowels. Any laughter that could be heard was hollow and phony—gallows humor—sounds that tighten in the throat.

Remember college initiation? The dean stood up and said to the incoming freshmen, "Look to your left, then to your right. One of you will flunk out by January." The Commanding Officers could have easily told these men: "Look to your left, then to your right. All three of you will be dead by tomorrow."

***

At precisely eleven o'clock, the final battle for Monte Cassino began.

The artillery barrage was like nothing even the battle-tested veterans had ever experienced. First, they saw it. The night was instantly turned into noon as one series of brilliant flashes was immediately followed by another, then another—the spotlights of war. The barrage was so bright that miles away one could use the light to read by.

A few seconds later the sound of it arrived—thunderous, ear-splitting, painful in its power. The entire Valley and hills shook, as if in fright.

The German paratroopers were witnessing and hearing the Overture to their own destruction.

Curtain up, light the lights, we have nothing to hit but the heights...

The Bohunks took a few last swigs from their spiked canteens, smacked their lips, felt their stomachs burn, and set off to hit those heights.

Within an hour, countless firefights were at full throttle, with so many fronts, so many skirmishes, that not even the Generals—with their neat little maps showing clean little arrows—could comprehend what was happening.

It was simply the end of the world. A quick flip, from trenches to hecatomb.

***

It wasn't long before the soldiers of each Allied nation realized that this battle was starting out to be an exact replica of those of the past winter. The same problems, the same unbreakable Germans, the same gluttonous mix of fear and death and insanity.

It was three minutes into the battle when the first ambulances were called. Three minutes later there were not enough of them to carry off all the injured.

There was no time for compassion, only time for self-survival. A Brit in a foxhole spent hours listening to a fellow soldier—wounded, screaming in pain for either help or the consideration of a quick death. The poor Brit could do nothing, *did* do nothing, only huddled there and listened and somehow brought himself to speak of it years later.

The Indian Frontier Rifles and Royal Fusiliers were charged with crossing the rivers at multiple points. Some of their boats had already been stashed and hidden at the river's edge, to avoid the nightmare hauling under fire that the Texans had had to endure in the first battle. But just like in that battle, the Indians' boats were being destroyed by artillery and swept down stream. The few soldiers who made it across walked into trip wires, mines, booby traps, and machinegun fire.

Everything seemed to replicate that old insanity, one more time, one for the road—keep performing the same foolish act, expecting a different outcome this time. Only this time, do it more—more men, more insanity, more deaths.

More of the same: Troops got lost and missed their assignments, either accidentally and purposely. Communication broke down. Even in the glare of the artillery barrage, guide wires could not be found to lead a path through the minefields. The wires had been cut, ripped by shells, covered with mud.

The land and roads had become somewhat spring-dried, but tank drivers once again were reminded that the battle tank is not an amphibious vehicle.

It could have been called another Chinese fire-drill of slaughter, except that the real Chinese were busy somewhere else, being slaughtered by the real Japanese.

***

Daybreak brought the first hint of a difference between this battle and those of the winter. Now the stifling heat of the Italian sun had replaced the freezing cold of the past. It was May in southern Italy and more men were preparing to die.

They were wishing they had written home more, wishing they had received that one last letter, hoping their corpses would be presentable and not embarrassingly truncated, making sure no awkward pictures or letters would be found in their pockets, letters from girlfriends that could drive wives into postmortem anger.

The enemy machine-gunning supplied the rhythm, while the shredded nerves of the soldiers supplied the dance.

Unheeded radio calls of: "Send in the buffalos (the tanks), we need the buffaloes," quickly changed to "Send ambulances, send medics."

By dusk of that first full day of the fourth battle of Monte Cassino, Allied failure had again ruled the field. Battalions had lost forty percent or more of their men. Tanks were sinking, rivers were turning red, men were dying as bravely as ever, and the Germans were the same old rock-hard pretzels.

Up on the ridge, the Polish Bohunks were dying at an even faster rate than the men down in the Valley. Last swigs of booze were taken, goodbyes were whispered from man to man. Point 593—that promontory steppingstone to the Monastery, that bump of land that had seen so many deaths over the winter, and had been captured and recaptured and then captured again—was once again littered with bodies from both sides of the battle.

Point 593 was achingly close to the ruins of the Monastery itself; more than once the Bohunks got the feeling that they were there, they were *really there* this time. They were so close they could almost reach out and touch the bones of Saint Benedict. But the bones were in the Vatican, and then the Germans counterattacked.

The Bohunks and the Germans played the same deadly back and forth game. Fog, smoke, darkness, and confusion left both sides disoriented and bewildered. Radios had been knocked out, the radioman was dead. Up on the Point, communication once again fell way to chaos: *Who's got 593 now? Do we have it? Do they? Where is it? Which way? Who's got it now?*

Few stopped to ask: Why do we want it? Why would anyone ever want any of this?

All senses and sense were relieved of duty. Poles and Germans were throwing rocks at each other, wrestling, punching, gouging, hurling curses when they could have been firing rifles, laughing, crying, or simply letting arms drop to his side, as one soldier did—he did not understand anymore—did not care anymore—was simply strolling away down the mountain.

Men were hearing clear orders to retreat, even when none had been given.

Same old shit. All over again.

***

Then…

Then…

Deep down below this chaos…down in the Valley…a bridge was built. A single bridge that made all the difference. No symbolism here, no poetry, I don't mean a bridge between man and man, conscience and action, or nation and nation. No, just a metal bridge. A bridge across a river.

And the bridge was called Amazon.

Working under the rain of shells that was pouring down, three engineering companies of the Fourth Division pooled their resources to build a single bridge. Heavy machinery operators had only their sunroofs and Saint Christopher medals to protect them, as they pushed dirt and lifted rock and dug ditches with their backhoes and bucket-loaders. These men were not killers, they were not even really soldiers—they were unarmed—they were builders. But builders die too, and many of them did.

Still, they kept pushing that dirt and ignoring death; 1944 sniper fire had replaced 1939 coffee breaks. Guys kept doing what they had done before the war, but now with bullets being delivered instead of that coffee in cardboard cups.

At one point a bulldozer operator calmly hopped down from his perch to do a minor repair on the engine just as a sniper's bullet ripped into the vacated seat. The repair completed, the driver pulled himself back up and in. Pushing dirt.

A bulldozer was knocked out of commission when shells shredded its track; the others kept working. Once the river bank was prepared, a pathway was laid for the Bailey Bridge segments to slide down into place.

Night came, the work continued, the Germans sent in green flares to better see their targets.

Some of the bridge workers went into shellshock—they began laughing, crying, sputtering nonsense as they worked; some just stood there, gazing, like pedestrians stopping to watch construction on a city street.

When the Germans saw the elements of the Bailey Bridge being trucked close to the river, they increased the intensity of their firing.

A second bulldozer was knocked out of commission. That looked like the end of the mission; these Erector Set pieces were much too heavy and bulky to be moved by hand. Then somebody remembered that tanks can push things too, and a big Sherman was commandeered to do the job.

The bridge plates were finally pushed into place, the ramps were fastened, and the bridge was completed. The artillery fire couldn't quite destroy the solid frame of the bridgework.

The bridge was open, ready for traffic.

Eighty-three of the two hundred bridge builders were dead, but the bridge was open.

The first Sherman tank of the 17/21st Lancers rolled across, followed by another, then another; soon there was a miles-long string of tanks, each moving quickly and irrevocably north.

From high up on the Massif, the Germans trained their field-glasses on the endless line of growling tanks; then lowered their glasses and looked silently at one another.

They knew that the Battle for Monte Cassino was over.

***

The killing continued, but killing always worked in favor of the Allies. Even though they were losing more men than the Germans, they had more to lose, so the Germans would run out first. In poker, it's called crapping out.

The Germans kept shelling the tanks, but for each one they knocked out, three more rumbled across the shaking but secure Amazon Bridge.

The battle was lost but not over. The men of the two American Divisions on the left flank hadn't sleep since the opening salvo; they were running on amphetamines and adrenalin. And dying. Their entire attack was not coordinated and was doomed to failure. Some of their officers—new to combat—were faking illness and heading back to the rear lines, to vomit and hide out.

Juin's French forces in the mountains started off with equally disheartening results, but finally managed to wear down the beleaguered Germans and break through their line. Most of the

Germans had been slaughtered, the rest were weak from starvation and had not slept for days. The French and the Moroccans were relentless; pockets of German paratroopers began surrendering their arms.

Finally, the Bohunks of Mother Poland—tired from the relentless battering they had taken the day before, but still fueled by patriotism and booze—were ready for one final assault on the Monastery.

Under their little pot helmets that looked like inverted candy dishes, they climbed the heights, using ropes to hoist themselves over the steep cliffs and hot rubble. They kept climbing toward the sky, toward heaven, toward the Monastery.

**

Inside the old Abbey's remains—which was by now simply a symbolic target—the Germans had been destroyed by days of artillery assault. Some had been reassigned further down the hill to stem various Allied advances. The smell of the rotting bodies within the busted walls of the old place was so bad that the two hundred remaining paratroopers were continually wearing their gasmasks.

Their position atop the Cassino ridge still offered the best view of the area, but the view was not a good one. They could see tanks still pouring across the river bridge, toward them. They could see that Route 6, the once impassible road to Rome, was now open for Allied traffic. They could see the wild-eyed Poles approaching with vengeance in their hearts and with rifles and bottles in their hands. The Bohunks had taken Point 593 one last time and everyone knew they could not be stopped. At least ten Poles were advancing up the hill for every German defender. But the Germans fought on.

Hand-to-hand combat was laced through with lunacy. Men threw stones and clods of soil at one another, or at no one. A tenor strolled along the ridge singing the Polish National Anthem, as if he were heading to the backroom of a bar in Warsaw. A few men simply sat down by the side of the path, watching the war as if watching a soccer match.

Few infantrymen were left in the Polish group; they had been reinforced and replaced by cooks and drivers and other noncombatants. It seemed that anyone with an ounce of Polish blood, anyone who had ever eaten a kielbasa, was joining the parade toward the Monastery, which was now nearly surrounded.

So the Germans left.

Some simply ran, some tried to surrender, preferably to the Ami-s—the Americans—or to the Brits, rather than to those vengeful and vicious Poles.

Some just sat and broke out a deck or cards, played until whatever would happen to them happened.

A few managed to make it back to German-controlled area, where they met old acquaintances who did not recognize them in their current condition.

***

After months of some of the most horrendous destruction of man and civilization ever experienced in the entire history of warfare, the Polish took the Monastery without firing a shot, and found nothing there but a broken and empty shell of a building. Filled with the broken and empty shells of men.

Fewer than twenty Germans had remained; and they were more dead than alive. If they had been in better condition, they would have been gone. They put away their playing cards and put up their hands. The heat of artillery and small arms fire was still choking the place like an inferno; but they were used to living in an inferno. They asked their captures for bandages; they had been stuffing paper and rags into their open wounds.

The Poles found closets and drawers storing nothing but corpses.

***

The Polish troops had forgotten to bring a Polish flag—maybe they had not been that confident. So instead they found a Red Cross banner, tore apart the red, and pinned it to a blue handkerchief. That was the best they could do, the closest they could come to flying the flag of Poland atop Monte Cassino.

***

Scooter: You can bet Petoola wouldn't have come unprepared like that.

Mack: He wouldn't have come at all.

***

The Battle for Monte Cassino had ended. With a whimper.

***

...Parade...Rest!...

Chapter Fifteen:
Johnny Comes Limping Home (Petoola Gets a Ride)

"Well I remember how on foot I climbed

The stony pathway leading to its gate;

Above, the convent bells for vespers chimed...

The silence of the place was like a sleep,

So full of rest it seemed; each passing tread

Was a reverberation from the deep

Recesses of the ages that are dead."

-from "Monte Cassino" by Henry Wadsworth Longfellow 1875

***

With the cork of Monte Cassino finally popped from its bottle, the Allied troops began pouring quickly north. Juen's French, rolling up through the mountains, had to wait for the slower moving English, as Canadian troops—after smashing through German defenses at Anzio—swung lock-step into the forward-grinding parade.

The Allies were now in perfect position to crush the entire Germany Tenth Army. The Germans were caught in the deadly pincers, with Anzio troops pressing in from the west and Petoola in the east with orders to use his Fifth—his best, his Blue Devils—to close the vice.

But Petoola had been worrying that he would be cheated out of a terrific photo op and an even better headline—"Good Lookin' U.S. General Leads His Blue Devils Into Rome," so he disobeyed orders, let the Germans wriggle free, and headed north instead (after combing his hair and making sure his medals were on straight; Rome was a sophisticated place).

In a war and a career full of controversial and intemperate moves, this was his most of both. With the British 8th Army pushing the German 10th back from the coast, all Petoola had to do was follow orders and let the teeth of that bear trap close. But by now he was so haunted by his distrust of the British, and so engulfed by his dream of leading a conquering army into that magical mozzarella-stuffed city on the Tiber, that he took matters into his own hands. He refused to accept a second place finish to these Brits; no silver medal for *this* cowboy—it would be gold or nothing for the Golden Boy.

As soon as Petoola disobeyed his orders, the trap sprang open and the Germans were freed to fight again. This infuriated the British; they got even angrier when they were told that Petoola had said he would have his men fire on the British army if they tried to get to Rome first, juking him out of the glory that was rightfully his.

***

Mack: See what I mean about this guy?
Scooter: Give him a break.

***

With the possible exception of that spiffy local lady who had called him a barbarian, Petoola's triumphant entry into Rome was all that he had been expecting it would be. The cheering crowds were out in the street with their tiny American flags. The press boys were snapping pictures and getting quotes. Marching bands were a bit heavy on the bass and tuba, but invigorating nevertheless. Faces were kissed, flowers were tossed. Tears of pride were shed. Bottles of wine that actually tasted like wine—having been saved for a special occasion—were uncorked. Congratulatory telegrams arrived with flattering messages from Washington and from high-ranking colleagues. More tears, rivulets of joy, and the ecstasy of achievement. Petoola had the giant "Roma" sign shipped back to the States for his own little private piece of the swag and booty.

And who cares about Cardinal Spellman any more, what that guy thinks—because now it was the Pope, *the Pope himself, the Holy Father, the embodiment of Jesus on Earth,* congratulating Petoola on his liberation of Rome. More grins, more tears, more kudos, more slaps on the back...

Not too many miles to the south, the bodies of thousands of dead soldiers lay rotting face-down in the muck of the battlefield.

A good time was had by all.

***

Now the Allies would have to fight the Germans again and again, all the way up to the top of the boot. Men continued to die as the entire Southern Campaign dribbled off the front pages and became increasingly irrelevant but still septic. The confrontation bogged down at something called the Gothic Line, a bit north of Florence, in northern Italy. The Germans had also set up a "Hitler Line" a bit north of Cassino. These guys were running low on troops and materials and ethics and time, but they had no shortage of name for lines.

Churchill's idea of puncturing the "Soft Underbelly" of Europe and then turning right at the Po Valley had proved to be little more than useless bravado.

***

Then came D-Day. The Normandy Invasion was launched just one day after Petoola's hero's welcome into Rome; the amphibious landing and subsequent battle immediately became the recognized tipping-weight of World War II.

This convergence of events—Rome yesterday, Normandy today—must have really gotten Petoola's ego percolating. He must have realized that from then on, no amount of personal public relations men or press corps scribblers or left-profile photographers could keep any emphasis on *his* army. It was all D-Day coverage from this moment until V-E and beyond; to the folks following the action from back home, the war was now a neat line being drawn west to east across the top half of Europe. A titanic ball game—Minor Leaguers from down south need not apply. That had been the Grapefruit League down there in Italy—Pre-season—Exhibition. Normandy and onward was the Big Time. The Show.

***

Not only bozos like me, but even the *real* historians agree that the entire Italian campaign was poorly conceived and more poorly carried out. It has been labeled by those who know as "The Worthless Campaign."

***

Scooter: How's that supposed to make *us* feel?

***

Sacrifice, slaughter, and stupidity. These had been followed by more…

Sacrifice, slaughter, stupidity.

The entire snafu, most agree, lacked any sense of sense, showed no imagination, and had no compassion for the lives wasted. The scribes and pundits who pointed this stuff out were writing about the Italian campaign, but might just as easily have been writing about war in general.

***

Scooter: What we saw and what we did, suffered through down there—it was worse than just "war in general."

***

THE MULES OF MONTE CASSINO

The argument that the Italian campaign served the purpose of diverting valuable German resources from other battle areas holds about as much water as those smashed and leaky boats that were supposed to carry you boys across the *Rapido* River.

For every German man and tank that was diverted, four or five of ours were also. The same goes for materials, supplies, planes, and military minds.

***

Mack: Well, maybe it did achieve *one* thing for our side. It kept Petoola away from any other battle sites. Can you imagine if that guy was running the Pacific? There'd be little Japanese guys with wire glasses and buck teeth raising the flag on Iwo Jima.
Scooter: That's racist or something.
Mack: Truman probably would've been dropping the A-bomb on Anchorage, Alaska, and Vancouver. "Petoola told me to do it."
Scooter: You've always been too hard on the guy.
Mack: At least he was down there with us instead of up in London, planning D-Day. "Forget landing crafts. We could teach the fellas to doggie-paddle across the English Channel. The Press Boys could get a shot of me wading on shore at Normandy—after it was safe. Just like MacArthur, but this time Me instead. And my Blue Devils right behind, of course."

***

As you can see from listening to these two guys, those lucky ones who survived Monte Cassino were often bitter and twisted.

***

Mack and Scooter: Who?

***

Post Traumatic Stress Syndrome hadn't been labeled yet, so many of the veterans had to wear labels like "shell-shocked" or "battle fatigued" or worse—"bomb loony." Each label carried with it a subtext of "Couldn't handle it," or "Wasn't tough enough."

***

Mack: Yeah, we weren't tough enough.

***

There was no celebration, no sense of pride, no accomplishment attached to being a veteran of this muddle of madness.

These men were offered little help, granted little understanding. Many were told they now had to ship up to France and do the whole thing all over again. Many had to survive the Battle of the Bulge after surviving the Battle of Monte Cassino.

***

Mack: At least people heard of that one—the Bulge, I mean. I mention Monte Cassino to people now, they look at me. "What's that, a wine? Some kind of gambling place?"

Scooter: The ads on the television say now that "The Battle of the Bulge" is watching your waistline, counting your calories.

***

The nightmares and night sweats went on for fifty and sixty years for these veterans—longer. Many vets of the Monte Cassino action finally found peace only in their graves. Men on both sides of the Atlantic drank, they cried into their glasses of booze, they abused drugs and family members. Some horrors are too horrible to climb over, they keep pulling you back down, every time, like the hands of your buddies pulling you down beneath the waters of the *Rapido*.

The Germans had it even worse, of course. At least our boys had won a war, a war that pitted good against evil, a war that had stopped the spread of Nazism across the face of Europe. Had put an end to the Holocaust. A lot of stories were written about the bravery of our men. A lot of cheesy but goodhearted movies were made.

***

Rivera (Richard Conte): Some of them not so cheesy, Pumpkinhead. Butt me.

***

In the movies, everybody on our side looked like Dana Andrews. Everybody looked like Petoola. Loretta Young was waiting at every door to welcome her soldier back home. But in Germany, the veterans just kept their heads low, tried to forget, and hoped their neighbors would do the same. Hollywood made a movie about the Nuremberg war crimes trial. Colonel Kling played a Nazi.

The German paratroopers who became prisoners of war after Monte Cassino barely noticed the difference in their daily existence. Although no planes were bombing them any more, and no one was shooting at them, there was still the sickness and the hunger. Just as during the battle, they would gladly eat a dead mule when they could find one.

Gli Sfortunati poked their heads out from the caves and from the collapsed cellars, looked around, noticed that the war had finally passed them by; they crawled back out onto the farmland that had been theirs for a thousand years.

***

Mack: Fertilized by the war, right?

***

Poisoned by the war. It would take a long time for the soil to turn back into usable farmland. The twisted metal was still hot. The mass graves held countless body parts that were not much cooler. Malaria held its ground, controlled the land, refused to move on, just as the stubborn troops had done in the winter of 1943-44. The fields still held hundreds of thousands of those buried, unexploded land mines.

The Order of Saint Benedict was now a homeless group of monks. For the first time in their lives, some were carrying doubts—Doubts. The ones who seemed most content were those who were allowed to die during the battle for their beloved Monastery, or what once had been their beloved Monastery. The sick monk who refused to join the procession down the mountain the day after the bombardment had stayed and closed his eyes; nothing against Saint Peter, but the monk hoped that it would be Benedict to meet him at the Gates.

Abbot Gregorio Diamare himself, the old Abbot, made it back to the ruins of the Monastery even before the war had ended. He said, "One day the world will learn the truth about Monte Cassino," and then he died in its ruins. 1945. Malaria.

The survivors of Monte Cassino—the fighting men, the peasants, the monks—
were all just that and little more. Survivors.

"What did you do in the war, Daddy?"

"I survived."

"Really? You did?"

***

The Generals made out better.

With the exception of that Congressional investigation into his conduct at the *Rapido*, things went well for Petoola. He was not meaningfully disciplined for heading up to Rome in lieu of doing his duty. Eventually he took charge of the United Nations forces in Korea during that conflict and represented the U.N. in the signing of the ceasefire. He got a fourth star for each of his broad shoulders.

After he retired from the army, he became president of the Citadel in South Carolina, the nation's oldest and most prestigious private military academy. He received the Distinguished Service Cross, the Distinguished Service Metal, and the French Cross

Legion of Honor. He wrote books and had highways and bridges named after him.

***

Mack: More than we ever got.

Scooter: I still think both you guys are too hard on Petoola. He was an American with a tough job, an impossible job to do, and he did it. That's all.

***

The Kiwi leader, Freyberg, went into politics back in New Zealand and worked his way all the way up to Governor General. Eighteen thousand of his men had been killed—per capita, the worst of any country—but they loved him still down there.

Even a few of the German leaders did okay after the war.

Freda vonSenger had a few rough years, got his hands dirty as a gardener, but eventually became headmaster of the Spetsgart School, and was content. These old military men seem to cherish a chance to live in the scholarly peace of academia after their military careers have faded.

As for those guys who had never even visited the battlefields of southern Italy, those who weren't even in the military, those who were really responsible for the entire campaign—the politicians—life went on, as Leon Redbone would sing, like "a Bittersweet Waltz."

Churchill continued to drink his expensive brandy and smoke his expensive cigars until he was an old man. He continued to lead his country and was beloved in England until his death in 1965.

FDR continued to give bloated dictation to his secretary and get re-elected.

***

Just as Saint Benedict had predicted, the Monastery was rebuilt for the fourth time. Today it stands as a major tourist attraction, an important stop on the tours of Italy below *Roma* and above *Napoli*.

Each detail of the prewar Monastery has been painstakingly and beautifully recreated. But it is a different place. Now it is a cemetery. Over twenty thousand men from thirty-four countries are buried there.

***

During the battle, some Kiwi troops had been sent up the Massif to relieve another company. They snuck up the hill in the dead of night in order to avoid detection and bombardment, and when they got to their destination they found the troops that they were suppose to replace to be asleep.

Not wanting to make any undue noise, or to disturb these poor tired souls, the Kiwis simply flopped down and went to sleep beside them. In the morning, they awoke to find that these "sleeping" soldiers were actually laid-out dead bodies. They had spent the night in a burial-dumping ground.

And that's what the Benedictines at Monte Cassino do now. They sleep beside the dead. They are an old and perhaps dying

Order—average age in the sixties, getting closer to heaven and to extinction.

***

Gli Sfortunati of Monte Cassino also now sleep among the dead.

The railroad station has been completely rebuilt, but it now faces a rusted-out army tank that sits in the middle of the town square. A young Cassino couple, about to be married there, joke that the workers are "polishing up the tank" for the ceremony.

The rental car outfit knows where the tourists want to go. First, of course, the Monastery. Then the clerk rattles off the directions to get to all the different cemeteries in town. Take the little Fiat sedan for an extra day and get over to Anzio, see the graves over there.

When I take my bus tours up to Monte Cassino now, I'm standing in the front of the bus with a microphone and a message. But my clients, in their Hawaiian shirts and Bermuda shorts, usually give me a blank look when I start talking about the battle. Some just look down, read their guidebooks, and wonder about supper.

The meandering cutbacks of the road up the mountainside are almost too sharp and narrow to navigate for Salvatore, our skilled but slightly reckless driver. The twisting road reminds me of the mule trails of 1944. You can almost see the animals and the tired soldiers trudging up and down on each side of the road. Their eyes are low and hollow; their shoulders are low and weary. They look at the bus and they wonder what we are doing here. This is still *their* place.

Like a line of tanks pouring across the Amazon Bridge, the line of tourist busses seems endless. The parking lot is a traffic jam explosion of loud engines and overworked mufflers.

The new Monastery stands before us.

The building itself still holds the whitish patina of new construction. It has yet to earn the yellowed glory of its predecessor.

The basilica is beautiful. In the 1980's an Italian artist created a huge and beautiful fresco, "The Glory of Saint Benedict." Did his hand tremble as he worked, shaken by the immensity of his undertaking and the importance of his task? Or did the hand of Saint Benedict gently grasp his, to calm and guide the brush strokes?

***

Mack: C'mon, give it up.

***

Although they no longer own the building—it is now the property of the Italian government—the monks can be content with the knowledge that most of their original riches have been returned, most came back from the Vatican storage, some from Germany and other spots around the world. A few pieces of artwork that had been stolen from the Abbey were found after the war—stashed deep within a salt mine in Austria, huddled in there for protection, huddled and hiding, like peasants in a cave.

So no matter what the name on the deed says, this is still the monks' building. Still the house of Saint Benedict.

We tourists feel that *we* must be the peasants now—*Gli Sfortunati*; we too have invaded this sacred building searching for a respite from the cruelties of the outside world.

***

Mack: Does this guy ever quit?
Scooter: Sweet.

***

Sometimes the sideways glances of the monks lead us tourists to believe that we are not even as welcome as the peasants were back then; but rather we are military invaders, forcing our way into a building that is not ours, for purposes that are not theirs.

***

Scooter: I bet the monks wish there was still a three hundred meter "Free Zone" to keep gringos restrained, at least that far away.

***

The monks tell us that the United States Government never gave a single *lire* toward the rebuilding of the Monastery.

***

Mack: Yeah, all we gave them was millions of dollars to rebuild the whole damn country.
Scooter: We were the ones who wrecked it.
Mack: The Nazis? Huh?
Scooter: Sure. But Germany was broke after the war.

***

The monks run the gift shop. Multicolor postcards and pictures of the Abbey in all of its glory, either before or after, sit in the wire racks, next to postcards showing the bombing and the destruction. The wartime cards are in black and white.

The tourist group heads out through the historic bronze doors—recast since the bombing—out into the surrounding fields. The hills, the fields, seem now to be nothing but cemeteries, one after the other. Thousands of red poppies grow in the fields and on the hillsides. Each flower stands for a man who died there. But there aren't enough flowers.

The British dead rest on the outskirts of town along with their Empire mates—the Kiwis, the Gurkhas, the Indians. The Germans are down in the *Rapido* Valley, the valley that they once had such a good view off, the valley that staved off their death, at least for a few months. The French and the Italians rest under the stones by the side of Route 6, the road to Rome. You wonder if the French would have preferred to be buried in the mountains, where they fought so gallantly and successfully. If we had listened to their beloved General Juin, much of the tragedy f Monte Cassino would have never happened.

All these men, I try to explain to the people in my tour, all those lives. I think some may be getting it now. The headstones are talking to them, making the point I can't.

Finally, the Poles, those incredible Bohunks, tens of thousands of them, buried up the hill a ways, near Hill 593, the little knob of land that they fought for so bravely and so many times. The inscription on their wall reads: "For our freedom and yours we soldiers of Poland gave our souls to God, our life to the soil of Italy, our hearts to Poland."

Finally the *turiste* head back to the building, using the same mule path that the monks used to carry their crucifix and suitcases and sorrow down the hill the day after the bombing.

We get back to the building and we stop to read the single word engraved in stone over the door, originally placed there by Saint Benedict himself: PAX.

***

Epilogue:
Mack and Scooter Jaw on War

"Jewels and binoculars hang from the head of the mule."

-from "Visions of Johanna" by Bob Dylan 1966

***

Scooter: Well, how do you think the guy did with the book?

Mack: Who, the Bozo? Henry? With *this* book?

Scooter: Did he get it right?

Mack: Doesn't matter. Walt Whitman? He was a pretty good writer, a lot better than Henry'll ever be. And he saw bloody war up close. Civil War, way up close. And you know what he said? That you can't put war in a book.

Scooter: He was right.

Mack: He was right. But Henry did okay, I guess. Henry's no Walt Whitman.

Scooter: Nope. But it's such a hard thing to get your mind around, your pen around. Jeez, the two of us were actually there, been trying for years, we still can't get it wrapped up. So yup, he did okay, I guess, considering. Did a little research, I guess.

Mack: I got the feeling he could've done more, but the books he was using were due back in the library.

Scooter: Good books he mentioned. I tried to read that first one, just couldn't do it. Painful.

Mack: What's it called again?

Scooter: Here. *Monte Cassino: The Hardest-Fought Battle of World War II.*

Mack: Got the title right, all right.

Scooter: A guy named Mathew Parker.

Mack: A limey?

Scooter: I think so. Amazing. You should read it.

Mack: Nah. If you couldn't get through, I couldn't. I don't read that much. Police reports. Wire blurbs. And what's the other one Henry used?

Scooter: I've got it here...Monte Cassino...*The Story of the Most Controversial Battle of World War II.* David Hapgood and David Richardson. This one's a little easier, mostly about bombing the monastery and saving all the artwork inside.

Mack: I guess those Krauts did one thing right at least. So, I don't understand, if this thing we lived through was the most hard-fought battle of the biggest war ever, the most controversial—all that shit—how come nobody's ever heard of it? I mention it to my kids, ask if they studied it in school…"Monte Cassino? Las Vegas?" they say to me. How come?

Scooter: Because the story doesn't make a good story. Not good guys against the bad guys. The Nazis didn't all wear a monocle and talk like Peter Lorre and were all maniacs. We weren't all…well…we weren't all what we should've been. Our side, I mean, not us personally, I don't mean.

Mack: Yeah, I guess. You know, it's probably best the kids don't know what happened over there anyway.

Scooter: You said the kids are good? Sarah and…?

Mack: Tom. Both great, both doing great. Yours?

Scooter: You remember, Lynn was pretty sick.

Mack: Yeah. How's that going?

Scooter: Good. Good. She's over it now, looks like. You ever think about going back there?

Mack: Where? Cassino? You mean like Henry does? Maybe take one of his bus tours?

Scooter: Yeah.

Mack: No. No. I have no interest whatsoever. You?

Scooter: No. I've done a pretty good job of putting all that behind. So now I figure—just let it lie. War, war memories, war is a sleeping dog.

Mack: It's a sleeping mule, war is a *dead* mule. Henry got one thing right, we were all mules, weren't we.

Scooter: Yes, that we were, yes. I think it was *you* said that, about us being all mules.

Mack: Oh, yeah? I thought Henry made that up.

Scooter: No, I think you did. That part was true, at least. I never felt sorry for us, though, for ourselves. We just got ourselves into it, what can you do.

Mack: Yeah, what we were called upon to do, just a part of living, that's all. War is as American as apple sauce and Santa Claus.

Scooter: Who said that? Rap Brown?

Mack: Who? *I* said it. As American as apple sauce and dental floss. Same way with the Krauts. Same way with everybody, I guess. All over the world. The Petoolas get themselves a hard-on, and us mules have to get it off for them.

Scooter: The only ones I feel sorry for—when Henry happened to mention it—the peasants, the farmers. Everyone I met over there was so friendly, so gentle in their suffering. You remember?

Mack: And they were the same way with the Krauts. What'd Henry call them? Glee? Glee club?

Scooter: *Gli Sfortunati.* The Unlucky Ones.

Mack: They were.

Scooter: Twenty million civilians, killed in Europe during that war. Our own bombers killed about five million of them. The RAF incinerated sixty thousand in Hamburg in one day alone, for no military gain whatsoever.

Mack: "Kids and cows." Lodge—he's a pilot I know, he's dead now, he used to tell me, we'd be talking, he'd say, "During the war I bombed kids and cows." You got the numbers.

Scooter: I remember reading. A quarter million killed in Japan, A-bombs, two days. *Gli Sfortunati ultimo.*

***

Hitler exterminated six million Jews in the Holocaust. We killed roughly that many civilians during the War too. Four million in Germany alone. Austrians, Rumanians, Italians. Not the same thing, of course not, but rooted in the same attitude: victims as mules, their lives not valuable enough to be considered in the bigger equation, the important stuff of how can we win, how can we move forward as a country, how can we achieve that nirvana that we all pretend is out there somewhere.

***

Mack: I thought this guy was gone already. Henry, you had your chance, okay? Anyway, I don't buy his point. He's making an equation you can't equate.

Scooter: No, but the mules do die. I mean the civilian mules.

Mack: (Makes explosion noises and indications with his hands).

Scooter: Does it change the bombing of the Monastery, make it any better? No. That's not what I'm saying.

Mack: Doesn't matter what you're saying. I'm not that interested.

Scooter: Well…

Mack: Along those same lines, you know what drives me nuts?

Scooter: Running out of free beer?

Mack: No, worse than that. How many'd we lose in the war?

Scooter: Americans? I don't know, about half a million.

Mack: And—speaking of numbers, here's a number I remember—how many of them were Generals? You know?

Scooter: No.

Mack: Eleven. Eleven out of half a million. That's not a big percentage.

Scooter: Well, there were a lot fewer of them to begin with, but wait, I got a pencil…it's point, zero, zero, zero, zero…two.

Mack: See? So, MacArthur says, "Old soldiers never die, they just fade away." But it's the *young* soldiers who…they never get to live long enough to just fade away.

Scooter: They should have made all of us all generals, we all would've lived.

Mack: I see these magazine articles, these news magazines, these television shows. They're about—I don't know—the Secretary of State, the President, the First Family, the Generals, all these studs down in Washington. All those high class civilians and the American kids are dying somewhere, somewheres off in the world. It goes on all the time. It's going on right now. The high hats make a call, and the mules start dying. So my thought is, how can these fuggers go bowling, work out in the White House gym, in the halls of Congress exercise room, go to their parties, go to state functions, when they should be tortured every single minute about that kind of stuff. Kids dying.

Scooter: Yup.

Mack: Okay, so you get elected, you get to go make the hard choices in the government, you get yourself the Big Job, the

Number One, that's what you wanted to do, finally you get it. But once you're in, and some choice of yours, some decision you make, it leads to kids dying, leads to the killing of the mules, leads to the death every fucken day of some non-combatant poor-ass in a foreign country and some American kids—then that becomes the only thing you have to concern yourself with, every fucken minute of the day. Okay, maybe it's something can't be helped, but then, you don't get to put on your tuxedo and go out to the opera with the movie stars. No Easter egg hunts on the White House lawn. Your wife does not get to wear a gown and show Edward R. Murrow around the White House.

  The rule should be this—when kids and children are dying at your hand, you spend years and the rest of your life tortured by it—you cry, go get counseling, you stay up in your room, you stay in your pajamas and your underwear all day, you don't go out, you don't have fun, you don't enjoy yourself, you don't smile pretty at the camera, until all your death work has been atoned for. No nights painting the town—people are dying, for Christ sake. There's work to be done. There's atonement to be made.

Scooter: I guess we normal people don't think of it like that.

Mack: Scooter, just suppose on your beer trucks, suppose you have to kill—I don't know—even just five drivers, a couple drivers each day. Let's say you're sitting in your office, you call in the sexy secretary…

Scooter: My secretary's sixty-years old, wears a housedress, flip-flops.

Mack: Okay, but still, you call her in, you tell her, "Agnes, we're gonna have to start killing five drivers a day, it's gotta be, it's part of the job." "For how long?" she asks you. "Long as it takes."

Scooter: I don't know, I'm thinking the union would object...

Mack: As long as this is going on, you're not...you're a human being, you got feelings—as long as this is going on, and for years afterwards, you're not going to sleep, you're not going to eat, you're not going to think about screwing...so, it's the same thing with the President, should be, any President, Democrat, Republican, Congressman, whatever—you stay in your room in your underwear, drinking coffee and sweating and thinking and crying—until all the killing is done, until you have stopped the murder of the mules. They're *your* mules, mules you were hired to protect, mules that you are responsible for.

Scooter: Well, okay, maybe someday we'll all learn that, someday they'll finally figure out how wasteful it all is. We'll get people at the top who won't permit themselves to deal in so much sacrifice, so much slaughter, so much stupidity.

Mack: No, we won't.

Scooter: Maybe it will be learned that—here's the beer talking now—that when innocents are killed, when innocence is killed—then atonement must be suffered.

Mack: Oh, yeah, you think so? Read the papers.

***

THE MULES OF MONTE CASSINO

Printed in Great Britain
by Amazon

57491404R00160